*An Astrological Study
of Psychological Complexes*

An Astrological Study
of Psychological Complexes

Dane Rudhyar

 Shambhala

Berkeley • *1976*

SHAMBHALA PUBLICATIONS, INC.
2045 Francisco Street
Berkeley, California 94709

© 1966 by Dane Rudhyar
Revised and totally reset © 1976 by Dane Rudhyar.
Published by arrangement with Servire, Wassenaar, Netherlands.
This edition not to be sold outside of North America.
ISBN 0-87773-085-7
LCC 75-10324

Distributed in the United States by Random House and
in Canada by Random House of Canada, Ltd.

Cover design by Brent Beck.
Printed in the United States of America.

To Tana

Who will live through the crucial decades ahead,
in the faith that she will participate creatively
and serenely in the birthing of the new humanity.

Contents

Foreword

IN THIS book I have attempted to integrate closely a modern kind of psychology and astrology. The discussion of psychological complexes and emotional problems proceeds fundamentally at the level of a psychological study of the whole person, and I believe it can bring to the reader interested in a fuller understanding of his and others' character valuable new insights regardless of whether or not he is a student of astrology. Yet astrology plays an essential part in the discussion and in this analysis of the causes and meaning of psychological frustrations, tensions and blockages, in as much as it provides a structural frame of reference enabling us to establish, as it were, a map of the psychic life of a modern individual.

Astrology provides the "structure," psychology the "contents" in this astropsychological study of human beings under conditions of stress and strain as well as in more basically harmonious situations; and, as I have often stated, these two factors, structure and contents, are needed in any thorough and inclusive study of all forms of existence, be they biological, psychological, social or even cosmic. The pairing of the planets Saturn and Moon, Jupiter and Mercury, Venus and Mars is part of an astrological tradition of probably great antiquity; but the significance of such a pairing has usually not been fully understood. The pairing has usually not been related to the basic functions inherent in every living organism, or even in any steady and self-perpetuating system of social organization.

Such a relationship is discussed in the second chapter of this

book, and a fourth pair of planets, Uranus-Neptune, is added to
correspond to a drive particularly intense in human beings, but
existing also in other forms of life, the drive for self-
transformation or self-transcendence. This is an essential urge,
presumably expressing itself at the biological level as "mutations," but becoming in man the great Promethean desire for ever
wider horizons, for the conquest of higher levels of existence, for
becoming "more-than-man" and reaching superhuman or ul-
trahuman states of consciousness—for becoming "God-like."

What the esotericist calls the "Path" is a way of self-
transformation and self-transcending; and this way can easily be
shown to include three fundamental stages—stages represented
in astrological symbolism by Uranus, Neptune and Pluto—with
perhaps a fourth one to be referred to an as yet unknown planet,
the probable existence of which I discussed many years ago, tenta-
tively naming the planet Proserpine. The study of these trans-
Saturnian planets, not included in the traditional system of astrology which we inherited from the Greeks and the Chaldeans,
would take several chapters and would have greatly lengthened
this book. For this reason I made only a succinct reference to such
planets. The significance they have in a "transpersonal" kind of
astrology has been discussed at length in my recent book *The Sun
Is Also A Star: The Galactic Dimension of Astrology* (Dutton and
Co.). In another volume, *The Astrological Houses: The Spectrum
of Individual Experience* (Doubleday), I discussed how their location in the twelve houses of the birth chart affect the characteristic
types of individual experience related to each house, and also how
such a location reveals the most significant way in which these
transformative functions to which the three planets refer can be
seen operating in the lives of individuals.

The ideas developed in this book belong to what, several years
after writing it, I called "Humanistic Astrology." The term,
humanistic, was used, not because of any relation to the European
humanist movement of the 15th Century—which later on developed as an anti-religious and ultra-rationalistic force in our
Western civilization—but in order to relate my astrological ap-

proach to the Humanistic Psychology movement started by Abraham Maslow, Anthony Sutich and many others. Just as Humanistic Psychology developed as a "Third Force" beside, on the one hand Freudian psychology, and on the other Behavioristic and Experimental psychology, so I thought of Humanistic Astrology as essentially different from the traditional fortune-telling and predictive astrology, and also from the recent research and statistical astrology intent on achieving scientific respectability.

This Humanistic Astrology had its origin in my book *The Astrology of Personality*, written from 1934 to 1936, and still now widely sold in its paperback Doubleday edition. It was further developed in several books, among them *The Pulse of Life* and *The Lunation Cycle* (Shambhala Publications), and later on *The Practice of Astrology* (Penguin Books) and *Person-Centered Astrology* (C. S. A. Press). What I have attempted to show in all these writings is, I repeat, the interdependence of a psychology dealing with the human person as a whole and of an astrology whose purpose is to assist individuals in the development and fulfillment of their total being at all levels.

It should be clear, however, that astrology and psychology can be of mutual benefit to each other only if it is well understood that astrological thinking is radically different from the rigorous intellectual thinking and empirical methods featured in modern science. Science proceeds by way of exclusion, dealing only with characteristics common to large groups; astrology proceeds by way of inclusion, relating every phenomenon of life to a few fundamental principles considered to be universally valid. The astrological planets (including Sun and Moon) are symbolic expressions of such principles. Because these principles operate at several levels of existence, the planets cannot be said to refer to *particular* cases, events or entities; they represent functions, which being common to every organized system, have only a *general* character. Thus, I have spoken of astrology as a symbolic language, as a technique of understanding, as an antidote for the exclusivistic type of empirical and rationalistic science dominating our collective mentality. It is a means to discover where the individual person fits in the universal scheme of life, the meaning and purpose of the individual's place and function in *our* universe— the universe our human senses and mind can perceive and therefore in which we can consciously operate.

Astrology can be a conscious way of meeting life's experiences and to gain from them understanding and wisdom. But it is only a means, a method—one among many. So is modern science only a means and a method, one among many. Each method has its value and it produces results at a particular level; whether these results are constructive or destructive, deeply significant in a human sense or only superficial and strictly personal, depends on *how* the method is used and *by whom*. I only can hope that the people who will use the concepts and techniques I have presented in my many books will do so, not for ego-enhancement, intellectual curiosity, or purely material and social advantage, but in order to become more conscious and integrated men and women ready to assist others in dealing meaningfully and harmoniously with their own problems and in actualizing their innate potential.

The Complex and its Origin

AS SO much in modern psychology, even at the popular level, turns around the use of the term "complex" and of what it stands for, it is important for the astro-psychologist to gain a basic understanding of the subject. To know intellectually what this or that complex means in terms of the psychological ideas of Freud, Adler or Jung is not enough. The astrologer should have a clear grasp of the process according to which complexes form and develop, of their original causes in man's negative approach to life and experience, and of their correlation with the four fundamental drives in human nature—drives which have definite and adequate representations in astrological symbolism.

The astrologer should also understand clearly how far he may be able to detect complexes through the study of a person's natal chart and progressions, and in what way he can use this astrological knowledge to help his clients, instead of (unwillingly) adding to their fears and their negative approach to life. In other words, he should be fully aware of the possibilities and of the limitations of astrological techniques when dealing with psychological complexes and all that relates to their development and cure or transformation.

The first task, in meeting the needs of the modern astrologer who seeks above all to be a psychologist and a helper of human beings, is to define the nature of the complex, as a general factor in psychology, and its origin.

The Columbia Encyclopedia defines the term "complex" as indicating "a group or system of ideas which originates in the mind of an individual as the result of an experience or set of experiences of high emotional content, and which is repressed from the conscious mind, but continues nevertheless to show its presence through the subsequent mental activity and behavior of that individual. . . . The more or less complete dominance of a group of ideas making up a complex over the mental activity of an individual gives to a complex its abnormal or pathological significance."

Carl Jung, to whom modern psychology is mostly indebted for the concept of "complex," defines complexes as "psychological parts split off from the personality, groups of psychic contents isolated from consciousness, functioning arbitrarily and autonomously, leading thus a life of their own in the dark sphere of the unconscious, whence they can at every moment hinder or further conscious acts" (cf. "The Psychology of Jung" by Jolan Jacobi, 1943, p. 35, etc.) Everyone has complexes. Complexes do not necessarily imply inferiority for the individual who has them; they merely indicate that "something ununited, unassimilable, conflicting exists; perhaps a hindrance, perhaps too a stimulus to greater efforts and so even to fresh successes." Yet they point out too "the *unquestionably weak place* (emphasis mine) in every meaning of the word." The origin of the complex "is to be found frequently in an emotional shock or the like. It probably has its ultimate basis, as a rule, in the apparent impossibility of accepting the whole of one's own individual nature."

I shall deal later on with some of these statements, but at this time the main facts to remember are that the complex is a group of set and unyielding "psychic contents" (ideas, feelings, sensations, memories, etc.) which have acquired a kind of solid rigidity and which are constantly adding to themselves similar mental-emotional elements according to a snowball process. Any complex begins with a particular experience, and grows in strength and inertia as similar experiences occur which the person identifies (rationally or not) with the first. More accurately, a complex originates in a person's reaction (either as an individual, or as a member of a group) to a particular experience; and any reaction to any experience can basically be classified as positive or negative—even though obviously the distinction is not absolute, and most personal reactions include both positive and negative factors. Yet one of these two categories of factors can normally be seen to dominate and thus to give a characteristic "feeling-tone" to the individual's response. In time, an attitude to life or at least to a certain type of event is built in which either positiveness or negativeness clearly predominates.

It is often said that an individual is "equal to the occasion." This means that as a new and as yet unexperienced event confronts the man, the latter has enough strength to meet its challenge. The momentum of the event and the resilient strength or power of adaptation of the individual are dynamically equal.

In order to grasp the full meaning of this, we have to realize that many natural events tend to disrupt the individual structure of any physical organism or personality. Life and individual consciousness or intelligence are precariously balanced within a field where intense forces of nature operate, ebbing and flowing according to the rhythm of vast cosmic tides that no man can control directly. Living organisms on earth can be killed by relatively very small changes of temperature; the body's heat needs only be altered some five degrees to cause death. Likewise, the functions of the individual psyche are so delicately balanced, and the development of an intelligent, harmonious, sane, vibrant and individually creative personality is such a "new" factor in evolution on earth, that any violent and unexpected event—a shock or "trauma"—can quite easily disorganize and injure the individual organism of personality. The more individualized and conscious this bio-psychic organism, and the greater the sensitivity of the individual, the more disturbing or destructive tend to be the shocks which he encounters in a world that seems essentially alien, if not inimical.

Man can resist successfully violent shocks, either if he is very tough and insensitive, or if he has great creative (i. e. rebounding) power. Toughness, in most cases, is only of the surface; and if the blow is sharp and straightly aimed, the near-animal organism,

once its hide is pierced, collapses at once. On the other hand, the
sensitive but creative person, while his or her power of recovery
may be great, has nevertheless to fight against an ever-increasing
inner fatigue. He is not killed; but he may become "weary to
death" of forever creating himself anew.

An experience of high emotional content is caused by an event
with great dynamic power; that is, an event which hits a vital
point in our bio-psychic organism—an important nerve-center of
our personal life, from which the blow radiates in many directions
affecting a great part of our psyche and our ego-structure.
Psychologically speaking, anything in our inner life to which the
ego has given a very great value (thus around which he has organized his patterns of response, of enjoyment, and his symbols
of meaning) becomes such a vital center. If the event destroys the
object that represented this value in the world of experience
(whether through death or disillusionment), a shock is the result.

Under this shock the sensitive and highly differentiated person
will either tend to collapse, or with tense fervor set himself to the
task of creating a new value. The less sensitive person may absorb
the shock with far less injury, but his rough psychic skin may
become callous from sheer self-protection. Under repeated similar
shocks the callus may degenerate into a hard tumor which in due
time may become malignant. In other words, the strong shock
aimed at a vital "center of value" in the psyche may have one of
three types of result (and often something of all three!): a disintegrative process sets in which, if it does not destroy, at least
tends to corrode the creative springs of the inner life—some kind
of rigidity and crystallization develops which eventually may turn
highly toxic—or the individual, setting into operation the inner
powers of his being, buries the dead and creates new values.

If one of the first two types of processes start, the bio-psychic
organism, sensing itself diminished and vanquished, develops fear
when faced by a recurrence of the same kind of event. On the
other hand, if the result of the original shock has been a deeper
arousal of the power to create new values and new goals, and thus
a strengthening of the victorious realization "I am I no matter

what," then *self-confidence*—the faith in one's ability to face any new crisis with triumphant creativeness—is established.

Fear is produced by the memory of defeat—whether this memory is strictly personal in nature, or is based on a subconscious memory of previous collective defeats. But we must differentiate between the objective fact of defeat and the subjective sense of defeat. When a man in a small boat meets a storm and while making harbor sees mast and sail torn by the winds, he is defeated by forces of nature operating outside of him and obviously so far superior in strength that he cannot dream of overcoming them by equal force. What he can do, however, is to tap within his inner life creative powers which, step by step, will enable him to adjust himself successfully to the outside impact of the storm, to deviate it or use it to his own purpose. In proportion as the individual uses his inner powers for a creative purpose he may be vanquished but not defeated; he experiences objective defeat, but does not develop a subjective sense of defeat and ultimately a defeatist attitude.

Here, however, the essential distinction is not only between objective facts and subjective reactions to these facts, but even more between placing the life-emphasis either upon meeting forces, or upon developing one's inner creative powers. It should be clear that, if in any life-contest between man and Nature the individual focuses his attention upon the meeting of his own consciously available forces and the forces of Nature, the picture he sees of the results of the encounter must indeed be dark for him. It is true that human beings by working in groups and synthesizing the recorded activities of many generations have succeeded in using many natural forces to their advantage and in altering their environment for more comfortable living; and today our civilization is very proud, and justly so, of its mechanical force-against-force accomplishments.

Yet a man returning from the last World War might well have asked: "Where has this led mankind?" It led to the worst condition of wholesale starvation, destruction, insanity and haunting fear that human history has ever known; and no one should be satisfied with the remark that, if Hitler had not lived, everything would have been all right. The tragic suffering of millions of human beings was not caused by any one man, group, or nation. It was the result of a collective attitude to life—a deeply rooted one—according to which human existence is seen primarily as a contest between forces, as a matter decided by laws of mechanics.

Where force meets force, there man must ultimately be defeated; the irresistibly moving forces of nature, either in the physical world or in the psychic realm of the unconscious whose depths are unending and unfathomable, will always in the long run defeat the forces of humanity, and especially of an individual person alone. Therefore, to believe that human life is primarily a contest between forces can only logically lead to a negative attitude to experience, to philosophical pessimism and defeatism. It must also lead to collectivism; for it seems obvious that the only chance individuals have to successfully oppose human force to the power of Nature is through complete cooperation and unanimity of purpose. Scientific materialism leads inevitably to social collectivism; Marxism to totalitarian communism.

Yet there is an alternative. Once we realize that the essential purpose of life for man is the progressive actualization of inner powers inherent in the creative spirit within the individual, the whole outlook is changed. There is no longer any particular importance or significance in the fact that the immensely superior forces of the universe are able to beat us repeatedly; the only fact with crucial meaning is: how much more of his inner creative powers is man able to actualize and to understand while struggling against the constant down-flow of nature. And as we deal here with the individual and his spirit-centered creative potentiality as an individual, Nature refers to social and generic human nature in his unconscious depths as well as to the natural forces of the physical universe.

A purposeless force-against-force struggle versus a purposeful training through the tests of individual experience in order to develop inherent creative powers in the field of earth-conflicts: these two interpretations of human existence may seem to the casual reader to differ only in a highly abstract and metaphysical way. In actual fact, the difference between them defines the most practical and the most critical issue which every person has to face, both as part of a society or group, and as an individual. This issue means today life or death for Western society; because picturing human life as a blind struggle for survival has generated a spiritual defeatism which is not only sending millions to asylums, but has brought Western mankind to the verge of destruction. Mechanized and atomic total warfare on a global scope is simply the concrete exteriorization of the psychological and intellectual attitude which believes human life (and indeed all life) to be a total, universal struggle between purposeless forces.

This attitude is at the root of all defeatism, social and individual. If a person with such an attitude to life experiences the frustration of any one of his highly valued instinctual desires— once, twice, three times—what reaction is to be expected except a negative one, a sense of defeat, a complex? He is weak; outer repressions are unbearably strong—so, what is the use?

Consider, on the other hand, an individual permeated with the belief that he is born in order to develop his inner powers through storm and sunshine, pain and happiness alike, and that the only superiority worth striving for is that which comes through a fuller and more effective use of these inherent powers, whatever the cost or the outer results. If he is beaten in any meeting with the mighty energies of nature (inner or outer) such an individual will not acquire a "sense of defeat," however bruised and hurt he might be, as long as he may feel that he has learnt and grown as a personality out of the tragic experience.

If the person considers his gain in subjective values and in creative self-development the one factor having essential significance this positive attitude utterly transforms what could have been interpreted as a crucial defeat. When, instead, the attention is focused upon objective losses in the man-against-nature struggle, and these losses are repeated again and again, no man can avoid feeling inferior and defeated. Such feeling is bound to color the next similar confrontations with life; the individual becomes incapacitated by his memory of defeat translated into fear. Outer conditions may actually have changed; he may have actually grown in strength; he could easily win this time. Yet, gagged by fear, prisoner of the complex, the man is already beaten before he even faces the new experience. He is beaten because he sees himself vividly as a puny, weak force confronted with a mighty opposing force which has become a cosmic entity, a relentless undefeatable enemy. Anything which makes him "see" his life-experiences in such a way is inimical to psychological health; whether it be religion, science . . . or the astrology which makes of some planets or aspects evil powers bent upon man's destruction!

It seems important to explain at length the manner in which all complexes are basically formed, however different their fields of operation, because it is only as one understands clearly their origin in a negative attitude to life that one can deal with them practically and safely, and search intelligently for signs of their existence through astrological techniques. Nevertheless, the astrological search for complexes and their roots, or for the probability of their development in the growing personality, is a very difficult one. It requires extreme care and the delicate weighing of "progressions" against "natal" indications; for, as in the case of indications of sickness or physiological unbalance of one kind or another, the astrologer is faced with the task of determining not what events are expectable, but how a person will react to these events. No event, no shock in itself can be said to cause a complex—and this is why Freud's "reductive" analysis through mere association of images, etc., should not be considered sound, or at least adequate.

Granted a forgotten event is found, to which, with the analyst's assistance, the neurotic can trace the emotional experience which has remained associated in his subconscious with the origin of the complex or neurosis, the important point is not that there was such a shock or "trauma," but rather that the individual *reacted to it in a negative manner*. Why did he react thus? This is the real problem to solve. It is a problem concerning his family, social, cultural, religious background just as much as his native endowment or temperament. No man lives alone, or faces life's confrontations alone and on the basis of his own experience and of nothing else. He faces love and death, pain and disappointment, emotional or business failure as a social person far more, in most cases, than as an individual.

Most complexes originate in childhood or youth; for then come the first shocks which catch the child unprepared or negatively conditioned by a force-against-force philosophy of life held by his parents or taught in school and college. How can we know, from a study of a birth chart, the kind of life-attitude which the person as a young child has imbibed, by a process of psychic osmosis, from his family and its cultural-religious beliefs and modes of behavior? What we have to discover in the birth chart is a pattern of bio-psychological tendencies, as well as a pattern of relationship to the universe in terms of the individual's "weak points"; then, as we watch the gradual unfolding of individual potentialities into actual characteristics of personality by studying the astrological progressions and transits (and all similar methods), we can to some extent see the child, then the youth, meeting his life-crises with whatever equipment his chart suggests is his by birthright. The combination of this equipment and of the crises of growth (their intensity and their timing) will tell the story in general terms, which in turn the astrologer has to interpret with reference to the concrete relationship of the particular person to his particular environment.

The positions of the planets Neptune and Pluto will have to be depended upon to give us very general indications as to the basic over-all attitude to life of the person's society and of the way in which he will be affected by it. The distribution of planets in angular natal houses will give us some clues as to his essential individual orientation to problems of selfhood and relationship. There will also be clues to the impact made upon the child by his parents, and to his behavior in experiences affecting the roots of

his personal being, his security, and the inevitable changes in his
relationship to his mother and to whatever represents for him an
external authority.

Here I should emphatically state that, where the exact time of
birth is not known and thus the cusps of the houses cannot be
determined, any valid analysis of tendencies toward complexes or
similar psychological factors is practically impossible. It is only
the framework of the birth-horizon and meridian that can define
the *orientation of* the individual to his life-experience. Whether
or not complexes will develop in a personality is almost entirely a
matter of orientation, and not a matter of events. The orientation
of an individual person (conditioned by his family and society)
toward any event that disturbs the bio-psychological balance of
his personality by striking at some of the main "nerve centers" of
this personality is the essential factor.

What an analysis of the birth chart should reveal primarily is
the nature of these nerve centers. It can tell which bio-
psychological function or functions constitute weak points in the
personality, and when these are likely to be spotlighted by the
individual person's need for growth and renewal. As these times
of crisis occur—either following the generic rhythm of biological
development which brings such crises as those of adolescence or
"change of life," or according to a purely individual pattern of
destiny—the weaknesses of the personality will be emphasized.
The time and the general circumstances of the crisis can be indi-
cated by astrology; but no astrologer can tell with certainty *what
the results of the crisis will be.*

As a complex is the end result of a crisis, in this sense astrology
cannot determine whether or not a person has or will have specific
complexes. It cannot even rightly try to measure somehow the
relative strength of the individual and of the life events assailing
him; for that would be viewing the situation as a contest between
two forces—thus, a negative approach.

One might say rightly that the majority of individuals tend to
follow such a negative approach to their own crises; and thus, in
most cases, they tend to experience to some degree a sense of

defeat which, if reactivated, will lead to the formation of a complex. But no astrologer can tell (at least solely from a study of the birth chart of an individual) that this individual will develop a negative attitude; for even the worst combination of astrological factors might instead arouse the creative powers of his deepest self and compel him to reorient his consciousness and his will in terms of the positive use of these powers.

If this be the case, though he be apparently beaten in contest with life, the individual nevertheless would be spiritually victorious. To develop a complex is to accept defeat at the hands of overwhelming forces. But for him who can see defeat only in his inability to grow, to learn and to actualize more of his spiritual potential, for such a person there can be really no complex—only fatigue. His attention is focused upon inner creativity, not upon the relative strength of his organism and of life-blows. He *uses* all life-experiences as pedestals to the creative demonstration of the spirit within. And a cross on Golgotha has proved to be a far more effective pedestal than wealth, social fame or personal happiness.

II

Complexes Affecting the Roots of Individual Existence

♎ ♏ ♐ ♑ ♒ ♓

IN THE first chapter I defined complexes as semi-autonomous groups of rigidly set and unyielding psychic contents (ideas, feelings, sensations) existing within the personality in a mostly unconscious condition, and able to influence or completely control the reactions of the personality to some particular type of new experiences. I added that the source of all complexes is fear and a sense of defeat or inferiority, and that these bio-psychological feeling-reactions to experienced (or about-to-be-experienced) events are produced when a negative attitude to life is held by the individual—an attitude based on his picturing himself as a weak entity opposed by far more forceful entities or natural energies, in a universe in which everything is decided by a sheer contest of strength.

Whether man regards himself as simply a physical body led by basic instincts, or as a bio-psychic organism controlled, as far as such control is possible, by a conscious ego, the fact remains that he is normally an organic whole; and the essential characteristic of all organic wholes is that their activities are motivated (consciously or unconsciously) by a few basic "functions." All organisms display functional activities, each of which takes care of one of the necessary requirements of the organism's existence.

At the level of the body, these functional activities are performed by specialized organs or systems, such as the breathing apparatus, the circulatory and nervous systems, the organs responsible for food-metabolism, the endocrine and procreative glands, etc. These functional activities of the body have corresponding psychic manifestations and overtones. We know them as the basic "drives" of the personal inner life; drives which either may be entirely dominated by physiological instincts, or may acquire new and transcendent or abstract characteristics by developing consciously at the mental level in at least relative independence from the unconscious and compulsive nature of these instincts. In other words, a man's basic functional activities at the biological level can become "individualized" and conscious, thus increasingly subservient to the dictatorial rule of the ego, king in the realm of individualized consciousness. They become known and evaluated as, or transformed into, emotions and concepts, ideals and symbols.

While there are but few basic instincts at the level of body-functioning, the related psychic drives can be developed and varied almost infinitely through the power of collective culture and social ideologies, as well as through the use of individual imagination. Imagination is essentially the capacity to transform biological instincts into a multiplicity of symbolic activities or significant images; to build intricate dramas, rituals or comedies (and as well, dreams) out of the substance of the biological, then social, acts through which the basic functions in man's life operate. One has only to consider the extraordinarily involved, subtle and far-fetched ways in which the basically simple theme of sexual activity has been expressed and developed through myriads of cultural and individual variations in order to realize how human imagination works.

The reproductive function—which is the foundation of all complex sexual activities, feelings, images and concepts—is, however, only one out of several basic biological functions necessary for the complete manifestation of the life-potential inherent in the human species. It represents only one of the basic needs of the human organism. These can be classified in several ways; but the most inclusive manner (for it takes in the psychological as well as the physical levels) seems to be one in which four essential functions, urges, drives, or channels for the use of energy are distinguished, as follows:

1. The urge to be a particular being.
2. The urge to maintain the characteristic form or temperament of this particular being.
3. The urge to reproduce it.
4. The urge to transform it according to some kind of purpose.

Each of these urges can operate in a positive and in a negative way: thus, as an anabolic or catabolic force. Each can, in its desire for satisfaction, spread over the whole field of the body-mind organism, unless it is checked by the other functional activities and kept within its place by the power that structures this organism. This power is fundamentally *the self*, if the self is considered as the basic rhythm and power that undertones all biological and psychological functions.* So conceived, the self constitutes a particular and essentially individual form of life-energy; but it is linked with—and, in a sense, it emanates from—a spiritual factor which, for lack of a better term, I shall call the Soul.

However, at the level of the consciousness of a particular person the structuring function of the self is assumed most of the time by the collective patterns of the society and culture in which the child is born. These patterns control the development of the consciousness of the infant, and together with the influence of the parents and of the environmental conditions of life they mold directly or indirectly, positively or negatively, what we call *the ego* of the child.

The ego represents the structure of the field of consciousness; it defines the way a person consciously and habitually reacts to the challenges and opportunities of everyday life. Though in its most obvious aspect the ego can be called a social construct, it also appears to the consciousness as its center, its ruling principle. Yet

---

*For a more detailed discussion of the nature of the self and of the ego I must refer the reader to my book *The Planetarization of Consciousness*. Ch. 3. (Harper and Row, N.Y. 1970).

it has only a very relative degree of permanence and it can easily become identified only, or mainly, with some function or emotional reaction of the organism-as-a-whole. A man says "I," and by that refers actually in most cases to the ego, and *not* to the fundamental power which sustains and guides the development of his total being—but which does so at an unconscious level. The "individual selfhood" of a man exists, most of the time, only at that deep level. What appears on the surface of consciousness— somewhat related to this essential individuality, yet usurping its true function without being aware that it does so—is the ego.

The "urge to be a particular being" takes a conscious form in man as the ego—especially in modern man. The ego seeks in any possible way to assert its being different from other egos; it adopts inevitably at first an exclusivistic approach to all life problems. In so doing it acts as any culture or society does, especially at the stage of tribal organization. It considers everything that is not itself alien—a dangerous "foreigner." There is no such exclusivism in the self, for while each self has unique characteristics, all selves can be considered as *overtones* of the vast all-inclusive *fundamental tone* of Man—and in a still broader sense of the entire universe.

The ego and its urge to be different should be referred mainly to Saturn, for Saturn is the principle which builds everywhere boundaries isolating the inside from the outside. Saturn means therefore the separation of the individual person from the larger whole of humanity—or even from any group within which this person operates; but Saturn also brings consciousness to a focus. It condenses and concentrates the consciousness, and without this focusing power of Saturn there would be no steady personal character, no society, no transfer of knowledge from generation to generation.

Saturn needs the Moon in order to act; for while Saturn is form, the Moon represents the life-contents gathered within, and structured by, this form. The Moon represents the capacity for organic adaptation to circumstances in terms of the particular type of response defined by Saturn.

Each of the four basic urges above defined relates to a pair of planets. The pair Saturn-Moon refers to the urge to be a particular being; this urge, when acting at the strictly conscious level, identifies Saturn with the ego. Yet in a deeper sense there is also something of Saturn in the self, for even the most open and spiritually inclusive individual is distinct from other individuals. But "distinctness" should not be confused with the sense of exclusiveness and unyielding difference which characterizes the ego, at least in the modern psychological sense of this term.

Jupiter, as we shall see later, essentially refers to the social sense, for it is thanks to the capacity in man for association and cooperation that man can preserve himself in the dangerous environment of the jungle; and our city-jungle is nearly as dangerous as the primeval forest. Jupiter is thus the preserver. It maintains what has been defined by Saturn; it does so in relation to Mercury which is the principle of relatedness, the power of association of sensations through the nervous system, and of association of images through the concept-producing intellect.

The pair Mars-Venus represents the third or reproductive urge—either biologically through sexual acts, or mentally through the projection of imagined forms (works of art, etc.) and cultural values. As to the fourth, or transforming urge, we can witness its operation in man according to the rhythm established in the sky by the planets Uranus, Neptune and Pluto. Each urge represents a special aspect of the life-force and of the psychic energy in man. Whenever the release of this bio-psychic energy is thwarted, deviated or dammed in, conditions arise which may lead (yet do not *have to* lead) to the formation of complexes; to each of the four basic urges corresponds a typical class of complexes, and it is these classes which we shall now study with reference to their astrological connotations.

The Saturn-Moon function is the root-function of any specifically individualized existence. Any living entity which can be considered as a relatively complete and self-sufficient biological and/or psychological unit must have limits, boundaries, and special or individual characteristics which make it "different" from other entities. This difference manifests in various ways and at various levels. A cat is different from an elephant; and the difference here is a difference between two genera, two kinds of animal groups. It is a generic difference, while the difference between two cats of the same species is an individual difference or rather distinction.

In the human kingdom we may assert that every human being should be considered as one whole species; while humanity as a whole is somewhat like an entire genus or class. At any rate, every man is characterized by generic (racial) and collective (cultural) differences, as well as by individual differences. Saturn symbolizes both types, according as a group of men or a particular person is considered. Every man has a "human" skeleton and posture, which differentiates him from other mammals; and this body framework is "ruled" by the generic Saturn at the strictly biological and unconscious level. But every modern individual has also an ego, which defines and limits the field of his consciousness and gives a relatively set structure to his conscious inner life; this ego is the individual Saturn.

Modern man, moreover, has established what he considers as the correct structure and pattern of all reliable thinking: viz., logic. Logic, as we know it in our Western civilization, is a culturally defined collective expression of the Saturn function at the level of mental activities. Yet every mentally developed individual ego has certain ways of thinking which are his own, inasmuch as they grew out of his own reactions to a relatively unique series of life-experiences. These "ways of thinking" may conform to the collectively determined patterns of modern man's logic, or they may differ from them in some particulars—an individual difference also to be related to the Saturn function, but in intimate connection with the Moon function which deals with the individual's capacity to adjust his mind to his own relatively unique life-experience.

When we find such individual differences in thinking and in the way in which the individual ego faces the events of his life common to all men, we speak of differences in "mentality" and in

"character." The more basic of the two are differences in character; for "character" (at least at the strictly personal level) should
be defined in this connection as the sum-total of the individual
traits of the ego—thus as the outward manifestation of the ego-
structure (Saturn) and as the individualized manner in which the
person adjusts himself consciously to his life-experiences (Moon).

By "character" we mean, thus, the personality of a man; that
which differentiates him from other men, and which he has built
through series of reactions to experience. When reactions to certain typical experiences *follow rigidly set paths which remain the
same even though outer conditions and life-needs (biological and
psychological) have changed,* then the Saturn function is shown
to have overwhelmed in these instances the Moon function of
adaptation. This shows that a complex has been formed. The cooperation between the trend toward individualization of character
and the need to adjust oneself to outer circumstances and crises of
inner growth has been broken. The former has repressed and
stalled the latter in some particular direction—and, at times, in all
directions. The Moon function has become subservient to, or
enslaved by the Saturn function.

This, obviously, can happen in two ways: either the Saturn
function grows stronger than the normal organic balance requires, or the Moon function becomes too weak as a result of its
having been injured by a shock or by lack of materials to feed its
growth. Every organic function develops normally through exercise and atrophies through lack of use or abuse. Moreover, any
organ and cell of the body needs special food if it is to discharge its
functional task. The same is true at the psychological level. The
biological-generic Saturn needs calcium to build a strong and resilient skeleton; and the psychological-individual Saturn needs the
experience of authority, of moral firmness—in short, of
character—in order to build a strong and resilient ego.

This kind of Saturn-stimulating experience is normally brought
within the field of consciousness of the young child by his contacts with his father. Likewise, the kind of experience best able to
stimulate the Moon function of the infant is gained through his

contacts with his mother, because the mother attends to his everyday requirements, adjusting her and the child's positions to changing outer circumstances (light and darkness, warmth and cold, etc.) and to the child's changing inner needs (hunger and disposal of waste-products; but also the need for enveloping tenderness and comfort in a strangely alien world).

In order to be a true father (that is, in order to meet the child's need for experiencing the characteristic Saturnian attributes of fatherhood) the actual father has to embody in the eyes of his child solidity, firmness, authority, security, rectitude, justice, morality, etc. Likewise, in order to be a true mother an actual mother must effectively demonstrate the characteristic lunar traits of devoted service and the ability to cope with all everyday emergencies, to feed the child's body with food and his psyche with tenderness, to provide physical rest and emotional comfort, peace and harmony, to act as *intermediary* between the conscious and familiar realm of the home and the disturbing outer world of dangerous things and unfamiliar or inimical human beings.

What the modern psychologist calls the "mother-image" and the "father-image" are built in every child's consciousness by his reactions to the way in which his mother and his father actually embody in his presence the above-defined ideals of the Father and the Mother—thus filling his need for having his Saturn and Moon functions stimulated and enriched by parental example. The child's consciousness grows by assimilating the living examples around him (by imitation). It may also develop, in case of hurt and deprivation, by rejecting these environmental examples; but then growth occurs under stress and strain, and complexes occur.

Saturn symbolizes the ideal father and the father-image in the child; the Moon stands for the ideal mother and the mother-image. Either of the two images can be so dominant as to weaken the other, and also the activities of the remaining basic functions. Either image can be negative and dark, obscured by fear, resentment or misunderstanding—or underdeveloped and dreamlike because of lack of real living contact with father or mother, thus leaving a zone of emptiness in the psyche, which some other function will try, inadequately as a rule, to fill.

In all these negative cases where the Saturn or Moon function fails to operate and develop according to the normal requirements (1) of generic human growth and (2) of the norm defined by a particular society and culture, a complex of one kind or another tends to form. Whether, as the process of youthful expansion in a social world goes on, the youth will actually harbor some typical complex with psychically destructive potentiality, or he will be able gradually to absorb and normalize the tendency to emotional rigidity, mental bias and compulsive unconscious behavior—this depends upon what life brings him as he matures further and how his other basic functions operate. In any case, his individuality and the particular structure of his ego-reactions will have been affected and to some extent molded by the quality and the characteristic outlines of his father-image and mother-image.

The mother-image occupies a primary place in the consciousness of the child, not only because the child is held within the mother's womb throughout the prenatal phase of life, but because the first great crisis of independent existence—the shock of being delivered into a completely unknown world and to have to depend upon some external source for sustainment (food, etc.)—deeply involves the relationship to the mother. Psychologists have recently given increasing attention to this birth-crisis (or birth-trauma), and to the possibility that the modern "civilized" ways in which delivery occurs (under some kind of anesthetics in most cases) and feeding habits are introduced may have some deeply subconscious influence upon the earliest formation of the mother-image. This is undoubtedly true, and the main point is that birth is the beginning of a relatively independent existence and thus of the consciousness of individuality—that is, of separation from the matrix in which the organism was rooted. From the psychic point of view, it is this sudden separation from the enveloping life and the uterine "sea" which causes the shock of birth. This shock produces vaguely conscious results, as the impression of separateness deepens through the repeated experience

of what it implies—mainly, an increasingly definite sense of isolation and insecurity, of lack and of organic discomfort.

The mother's feeding, care and caresses—the warmth of her
body which no doubt reawakens the memory of the intra-uterine
state and brings reassurance—tends to counteract and neutralize
the baby's feeling of fear born of isolation. Isolation is at first
organic and physical; but gradually psychological overtones will
develop. The physical "break" from the mother's womb is paral-
leled later on by a psychological break from the mother's
psyche—by what Dr. Kunkel calls the breakdown of the "primal
We," the feeling of identification between mother and child.*
This psychic separation is probably the most important crisis at
the psychological level, and the more familiar type of mother-
complex derives from it.

Separation from the mother, either at the biological or psychological level, poses problems of adaptation to the physical or the
psychic environment. And it is when faced with such problems
that the child looks to the mother (or anyone taking her place) as
to an exemplar. When the exemplar proves inefficient or moves
surrounded with fearful shadows, the mother-image turns dark;
and the child's own lunar function of adaptation to everyday life
becomes negative. He approaches life-experiences with a defeatist
attitude, with fear—or later perhaps, as a violent compensation,
with aggressiveness.

The father-image is less primary than the mother-image, because the father is more remote in biological experience for the
new-born. The father's function becomes clearer to the child
when he learns of an "outside world" beyond the limits of his
home; already the father-image carries the implication of social
behavior. Saturn, likewise, is far more remote than the Moon,
whose changing light adequately symbolizes what the child must

---

*Dr. Fritz Kunkel was at first a disciple of Adler, but while in America during
World War II, leaned increasingly toward Jung. He wrote several valuable
books: *In Search of Maturity, Creation Continues, Dear Ego,* etc. (Scribners,
N.Y.).

consider strange and inexplicable changes of moods and of love-attitudes in his mother, according to the time of the day and to other, to him, puzzling circumstances; and Saturn has a close relationship to Jupiter, which is the basic symbol of all social and associative functions.

Before we come to study the various kinds of complexes derived from the father- and mother-images, I should bring to the reader's attention the fact that while the pair Saturn-Moon symbolizes the father and mother, there is also an essential polar relation between the Sun and Moon. This solilunar relation expresses the dynamic bi-polar nature of the life-force itself which animates both the biological and the psychological organism; and it is to it that we must refer the fecundative act which is the source of organic existence and produces the embryo. The male sperm polarizes a solar force rather than a Saturnian principle. And in the prenatal life, Saturn is hardly effective, only as bone-builder; and bones are yet very soft.

Saturn's power begins as the biological organism is ready for individualization; when therefore the roots of the ego begin to develop. This occurs, first, at birth; then, in a new way, at the time when the "milk teeth" (born of mother substance—symbolically at least) are superseded by permanent teeth, Saturnian teeth; thus, around the age of seven. While the intra-uterine prenatal period sees the development of the Moon function (the power to exist in an outside world as an independent organism adjusting itself perpetually to circumstances), the first seven years of the life represent a corresponding "gestation" of the Saturn ego.

Around seven, the father-image becomes definite and concrete—then begins the formation of father-complexes if the image develops in a negative way. When earlier well-defined father-complexes occur in girls, they do not refer to Saturn as much as to the Sun; for the actual father can also polarize the man-lover image for his daughter, an image symbolized in a woman's chart by the Sun. This is a very important distinction, which must not be forgotten when we seek to refer a father-complex in a girl's life to a natal planet. In the boy's life the Moon represents the mother as an embodiment of both the mother function and the woman-image—another highly significant fact, which I shall touch upon as indications of parental complexes in astrological birth charts are being discussed.

III

Mother and Father
Complexes

AND THE TWO APPROACHES
TO ASTROLOGY DERIVED FROM THEM

IN ORDER to develop these Saturn-Moon functions in himself, the new-born child, confronted with the necessities of independent existence in a totally unfamiliar and dangerous world, looks to his parents for an example and model. They become intermediaries between the world and his slowy unfolding inner psychomental powers; they channel the age-old experience of man into his own consciousness and nascent ego; and they protect him until the development of his Saturn-Moon functions is advanced enough for him to meet all normal life-experiences with average chances of success and on the basis of his more or less individualized self.

To be an intermediary and shock-absorber, an exemplar of effective human behavior, and a protector—these are the three essential roles of both the mother and the father in relation to their child. By fulfilling them satisfactorily they insure the normally successful development of the Saturn-Moon functions within the child's psyche, that is, of his individuality and adaptability to his inner and outer environment. Failing to do so for one reason or another, the parents unconsciously force the child's Saturn-Moon functions to grow under stress and strain or without the proper psychic sustainment. Improper functional balance is the result. The mother-image may be so insistent as to leave the father-image in the shadow, or vice versa. Either of these may remain undeveloped through lack of parental example, guidance and love—love meaning here an unconscious transfer of psychic energy-substance from the parent to the child, which calls forth a response stimulating the corresponding function in the child.

A zone of psychic emptiness (an atrophied function) compels in turn another function to overdevelop in an abnormal manner; and the disturbance means that, when the youth faces a life-situation calling for the exercise of the undeveloped function, he feels himself inferior to the occasion and lacking in usable dynamic power. He has to meet the event with an unfocalized will, mind or ability to feel (thus, in an immature manner), or with a disabled organism. His tendency is then to come to the meeting with a negative and defeatist attitude, as a weak force facing an overwhelmingly strong power. He is so shocked or dismayed by his weakness that all he can see is a struggle between two uneven quantities or forces. He is unable to concentrate on a positive approach to the experience; that is, on the development of the quality of his own individuality through the experience, whether this experience results in what people call success, or in pain and inner retreat.

The popular idea of a mother-complex is that it expresses an exaggerated attachment to and dependence upon the mother. This is only partly true, for one can speak as well of mother-complex if a youth, having lacked a mother's love and guidance (whether the actual mother was around him or not), is forever seeking to fill in one way or another the inner emptiness which this lack produced. This occurs also if the youth, having been deeply hurt by and resentful against his mother, is having a portion of his psyche blighted by the resulting shadow, unconscious though he be of actual bitterness.

If the child's and adolescent's need for a mother was largely unsatisfied, the tendency is for the youth to transfer the unfulfilled longing from the concrete mother who has proven inadequate to her task of feeding and stimulating his Moon function, to a transcendental image of motherhood. Such an image will seek embodiment or substantiation; every ideal and desire always does so. It can find it in a universal or collective factor, such as the soil of his native land, the sea, the Church, a faith-compelling and quasi-religious Party (like the Communist Party), or any social humanitarian Cause which enfolds psychically the youth as a transcendent "womb," as well as provides an inner sense of security, the emotional stimulation of companionate relationship, and guidance of some sort (whether it be the dogma and the leaders of the faith, or the cosmic rhythm of seasons, that do the guiding).

Even faith in astrology can represent a transcendentalized mother-image, for the sky can be an unconscious substitute for the enfolding mother, and the cycles of the planets can be seen as a universal protective and guiding influence, which "mediates" between the chaos of earth-events and the ego frustrated in the development of its Moon function. Here, however, more than the mother function is implied, for as soon as the sense of universal order and cosmic Law is stimulated, the father function is also involved. Likewise, as Catholic apologists have often stressed the Church is the spiritual "Mother," but the Law of God and the Prophets (and the pontiff's authority which enhances the administration thereof) is a transcendent expression of the father-image.

As in early child-life the mother hides within her loving care, and at the same time reveals, the authority of the paternal principle of Law, so the universal Great Mother—in the bosom of whom mystics and men yearning for "cosmic consciousness" seek to lose their unfulfilled or surfeited sense of form and individuality (Saturn function)—hides and reveals the Will of God. Whoever rhapsodizes about fulfilling either his or her destiny, or God's Plan, demonstrates a transformation of his father-image into a cosmic Law (symbolized by the cycles of celestial bodies) or a Saturnian Law-giver, Jehovah-God. And whoever extols the "communion of the Saints" or a "religion of humanity" reveals a collectivization and extension of his mother-image, behind which can be seen the outline of a universalized Father principle.

Indeed the Great Mother and the Universal Father can take a vast variety of forms at several levels. It would be a grave mistake

to say that these many forms are "merely" expressions of mother-
and father-complexes—in the sense in which we are using here
the term, complex. The universalization and transcendentaliza-
tion of the mother and father functions are not only valuable, but
essentially necessary processes in the over-all evolution of man's
inner powers and consciousness.

The biological must be raised to the mental-spiritual, in order
to meet the descent of creative spirit which is a universal "ideo-
dynamic" factor. We may think of this "raising" as an ascent
from one octave to the next—and some astrologers are fond of
using this concept of octave, which means level, when discussing
the characteristics of the planets. We may refer it to the yogic
ideal, in India, of the raising of Kundalini from the root of the
spine (Saturn center) to the head (the transcendent Moon center,
which becomes a chalice to receive the spiritual downpour of divine consciousness via the Thousand-Petalled center representing
"astrally" the myriads of convolutions of the brain). But, under
any of a multitude of names and images, the same reality is
meant.

What differs is the relative degree of emphasis placed upon the
Father- and the Mother-principles—and, as well, on the "ascent"
and the "descent." In India, the Mother-principle has been emphasized, in practice if not always in theory; and the process of
ascent of the personal to the universal has been studied in all its
aspects. In the West, on the other hand, with the Jewish and
pre-Jewish tradition to which Christianity has become an heir, the
Father-principle is greatly stressed, and so is the process of descent of the spirit (Prophethood in the Old Testament, the Pentecost in the New). Jehovah is a Saturn-God, and Jesus referred
constantly to his Father in Heaven.

Exoteric Buddhism (as publicly known) and the Tantric systems in India are polarized by a basic approach to the Great
Mother, whether considered as Nirvana or as universal Power.
Gautama the Buddha, it is true, taught to the few, and
exemplified in his life, severance from the typical Mother-pattern
of India. Moved by total compassion for all sentient entities, he

gave up the Nirvana-state, giving thus to compassion the character of a supreme Law in which the Father-principle (Law) and the
Mother-principle (Love) find themselves synthesized. Yet what
his followers made of his teachings has remained pervaded with
the transcendental Mother-image, even in spite of the rationalistic
technique and the ascetic ideals emphasized.

The universalization of the Mother-image is the typical product
of the vitalistic stage of human philosophy, a stage in which "life"
is the object of worship, and all forms of fecundity and all expressions of the life-force are venerated. The vitalistic approach to life
and the various cults of fertility derived from it flourished in, and
consciously or not, still form the basis of all agricultural civilizations stressing the ideal of cultivation and multiplication of the
seed. It is in such civilizations—ancient Chaldea, China, North
India, Egypt, and America—that astrology was developed, at
least as far as we can trace its origins. Indeed, the whole zodiac
(the equatorial "Belt") is a universal matrix; the 12 Zodiacal
Hierarchies ("Souls" of the 12 signs) represent the differentiated
formative powers of life, operating in every organism. And the
astrological universe is an organism; even "events" are considered in horary astrology as organic wholes being born, developing and disintegrating. The whole of astrology is an attempt to
universalize the Mother function in man and to rationalize it by
seeing through it the Father-principle (order and intelligence) at
work as a dynamic creative impulse or pattern.

All of this is perfectly sound psychology, as long as the father
and mother functions are well balanced in relation to each other.
Complexes occur only when one of the two overwhelms the other,
and when, as a result, the individual finds himself inferior in the
exercise of the underdeveloped and frustrated function; and this
gives us a new slant on ascertaining the degree of psychological
wholesomeness in an individual's approach to, and use of astrology.

Where astrological practice emphasizes the force-character of
planets considered as entities actually releasing good or evil "influences," there we find behind it both a dominant mother-image

and a negative "force-against-force" attitude to life. Whoever uses astrology in that way betrays a psychological mother-complex—that is, an unconscious and at least partly irrational dependence upon a Great Mother. The individual stresses "fate," and shows an underdeveloped sense of individuality and "form"—a frustrated or weak father-image and Saturn function.

The mother function, I repeat, is essentially the capacity to adjust one's bio-psychic organism to circumstances and life situations. The individual with a mother-complex based on over-attachment to his actual mother shows himself dependent upon his mother for his day-by-day adjustments to the demands of his environment. His mother either has to tell him what to do, or, in a subtler way, she controls by her example and psychic influence his responses to life-experiences, particularly where women and the use of his creative powers are concerned.

If, however, the mother-image being weak and the individual's function of adaptation (Moon function) having been starved or frustrated by an ineffectual or absent physical mother, the individual has transferred his yearning for mother-guidance and mother-example to a universalistic level and become a devotee of astrology, what happens is that now he depends upon astrology (to him the great universal Mother-principle in celestial operation) for the very same type of guidance which a youth over-attached to his physical mother demands from her. This type of maternal guidance is both specific (i.e. dealing with particular concrete problems of adjustment to outer and inner surroundings) and charged with feeling contents. Quite frequently it is irrational, because it is emotionally biased and determined by personal reactions to personalities who either are good or bad, liked or disliked "at first sight" (the so-called "woman's intuition").

In astrology, this kind of "motherly" guidance manifests as the popular attitude according to which astrology is called upon to solve concrete problems, to pass emotional judgment on situations or people, to determine good or bad periods for doing things, etc. In other words, astrology is called upon to replace the individual's inner capacity for valid and successful adaptation to new

life-situations. This means nothing short of psychological dependence upon a mysteriously all-wise celestialized Mother who has
a safe, protective and adequate advice to take care of every practical need. To feel the need for such a concrete and habitual guidance is the sign of a transferred mother-complex—however slight
it be.

This does not mean, let me say at once, that astrology cannot
be legitimately called upon by normal, psychologically positive
and mature persons to solve some of their personal problems! The
task of solving problems posed by life-situations can be met, however, in several ways, astrologically as well as psychologically
speaking. The person should use both his mother-powers (Moon
function) and his father-powers (Saturn function); that is, he
should use a balanced combination of his power of adaptation to
life and his capacity to be an individual person, formed and
steady.

To approach one's birth chart from the father function point of
view means to see it as a "structural whole," as the symbol of
one's total individual selfhood. It is a "holistic," integral, qualita-
tive approach. On the other hand, to stress the dynamic "influence" of personalized celestial entities (planets and the like) as
these play one by one upon one's unsteady and easily affected
organs, feelings and moods, is to approach astrology as a child
seeks his mother. The child depends upon his mother's specific
and concrete guidance because he is inherently weak and his individual ego is as yet unsteady and immature. He is a weak force
facing frighteningly powerful life-energies or utterly confusing
life-situations. He must seek guidance and ways of circumventing
what he dares not face. This is a negative approach, which, while
it is inevitable in actual childhood, leads to the formation of a
mother-complex when prolonged past the formative years of
adolescence.

To meet astrology in a positive, mature and truly individualized manner is to seek from it:

1. A more complete knowledge of the "structural law"
(Saturn) of one's individual selfhood;

2. A fuller grasp of inter-functional relationship;

3. A means to focus more precisely one's conscious attention upon any particularly difficult problem or situation, thus enabling one to analyze more objectively and accurately the nature of all the factors it embraces, with reference to both society and one's own individuality.

This positive approach is based upon a mature and independent capacity for form-analysis; upon the conscious knowledge of cycles and cyclic structures; upon an objective and positively focused interpretation of symbols and of all the basic qualities and functions inherent in the state of individual existence. It is possible only when the Saturn function is adequately developed, in close and harmonic association with the Moon function.

If the Moon function is overstrong, the objective structural grasp of the situation, as pictured by the astrological chart or charts, dissolves into a sense of confusion and of dependence upon guidance born of the fear of *forces* which seem overwhelming. If, on the other hand, the Saturn function has developed at the expense of the Moon function, the theoretical and technical power of objective analysis (Saturn) so dominates the faculty of immediate adaptation to concrete life situations (Moon) that the astrologer becomes lost in theories and formulas about self and universe, cycles and abstract patterns . . . and fails to see the practical solution required to meet more successfully the immediate personal need. He therefore finds his approach to astrology vitiated or crystallized by a father-complex. He is overanxious to discover perfect order, an all-encompassing universal or divine Plan, and his "place of destiny" in a rationally structured world of pure concepts and cosmic qualities, *because* he senses in himself disorder, confusion, or vast irrational tides of a life too strong to be mentally grasped. He seeks clarity and form at all cost, and refuses to meet immediate concrete problems (Moon function) unless he rationally understand them and sees definitely his place in relation to them (Saturn function). In other words, the Father-principle is not normally developed in his psyche, having not been fed and stimulated adequately by a physical father. He therefore seeks everywhere for a transcendent Father—be it God or a cosmic Law.

If his actual father has been overpowerful and tyrannical, the individual may have another kind of father-complex; he will tremble before authority and feel unable to call his individuality his own. He will see in his birth chart a rigid, unevolving pattern holding his every feeling and act as in a vise. He will face life with dogmas, situations with set rules, love with ethical precepts. In him, the source of spiritual creativeness will have become utterly dry.

A whole book could be written on describing the various ways in which mother- and father-complexes can and do manifest in the lives of individuals; and modern psychological textbooks are full of examples which anyone practicing astrology with the view of proffering psychological assistance should carefully study. I can only stress here a few essential points. What the astrologer seeking for indications of complexes in the chart of an individual must never forget is that *any complex is produced by the abnormal development of one of the basic functions in the bio-psychic organism of personality*. But "abnormal development" may mean over- or under-development; it means, above all, unbalanced growth of the function.

Astrology, by pairing planets according to polarity, gives us an excellent way of evaluating this factor of unbalance. Wherever one of two polar planets—such as Saturn and the Moon—appears far stronger than the other by position in sign and house, or through the aspects it makes within the whole planetary pattern of the birth chart, a tendency toward a complex, affecting the basic function represented by the two planets, can be expected. The "tendency" only, let me emphasize. This tendency may not show forth actually until progressions and transits bring it out, whether in youth or old age. Indeed, it may not manifest as a definite and strongly inhibiting complex if other functions can absorb the strain and stress caused by the unbalance.

As Jung and Adler have pointed out constantly, a complex can act as a lens focusing psychic energy in a definite (though usually too rigidly set) direction, and thus lead to outstanding personal achievements. These may be great creative and spiritual achievements, provided it is the spirit that uses and acts through the complex, and not the complex which, as a "partial personality" split from the total individual being, uses the twisted energy of life to project its disequilibrated and fragmentary consciousness upon the outside world. In the first case we may have a great religious leader, law-giver, empire-builder, artistic or scientific genius, whose creativeness the Freudian psychologists love perversely to analyze away as the "mere" product of complexes. In the second case, we have the individual with unsocial, negatively stimulating, anarchistic or criminal tendencies. The former embodies a mutation in the evolution of mankind; the latter is a catabolic or degenerative force which ultimately destroys itself as well as what it touches.

IV

Astrological Indications of Father and Mother Complexes

NO BIRTH CHART can given the complete assurance that the native displays a mother-complex or any other complex. It can show unbalance in polar functions, tensions developing between normally complementary energies in the body and the psyche, emphasis caused by strain-producing circumstances of one kind or another, especially stressful crises of growth and their at least approximate timing. But the astrologer can only determine tendencies, and at best their relative strength. He cannot ascertain what the actual life will be as a result of such tendencies, even if they should appear as strong complexes; for no one can tell from a study of birth chart whether the individual will be a weak neurotic living an unnoticed and meaningless life tyrannized by complexes, or will be able to transform the rigid psychic structures of the complexes of childhood and adolescence into a lens or any other kind of psychic apparatus *through which* the spirit can act, and so acting, move human society.

By "spirit," here, I mean either the "individualized" spiritual Entity responsible in a transcendent manner for the birth and development of the personality as a whole or a "collective" racial or generic Power that uses the personality (and its neuroses or psychoses) in order to affect, constructively or destructively, a social group, a nation or the whole of mankind.

Anyone seeking honestly to correlate the findings of astrology and those of modern psychology is obliged to admit that there can hardly be any point by point correspondence between the two. No one astrological factor represents any one complex; no one particular planetary position or aspect can tell us whether a person is an introvert or an extrovert. Indeed, the greatest difficulty for the modern "scientific" mentality in acknowledging the validity of astrology is that any astrological factor can mean a large variety of things, and that any psychological characteristic or happening can be represented by various astrological factors or combinations of factors.

The scientist (and the modern psychologist usually tries to be a scientist in his field) proceeds in his work by a technique of analysis and exclusion. Whether he speaks of the mother-complex and of a psychological disturbance like schizophrenia, names a physical disease under which a variety of symptoms are covered, or calls any cat a representative of the biological family *felidae*, the scientist makes his definitions by considering a number of concrete phenomena which appear similar. At the same time he eliminates those that are not common to the group. The common features are then stressed as characteristics of a class of phenomena to which he gives a name. The name represents what is precisely common to the group of phenomena, entities or events; and what is not common is at least temporarily dropped out of sight and called secondary individual traits eluding scientific inclusion in the group.

Astrology, considered as a typical approach to life and meaning, operates in an entirely different manner. It does not start with concrete phenomena or entities, but instead with *functional qualities and structural patterns*. These qualities of being, or "archetypes," are seen as dynamic centers of functional activity in any organism, system of events or conceptual whole. Each center of activity is defined *in relation to* other centers and to the whole. As to the concrete phenomena which the scientist observes, these, for the astrologer, partake of the characteristics of several or all of these centers of activity. Every quality (every planet, sign, house, etc.) is *included* in every event or entity.

In other words, when the psychologist speaks of a father-complex of a particular kind, he has in mind a definite set of psychological characteristics which can be found in all father-

complexes of this kind; and having in mind this set of characteristics, he *excludes* automatically all "secondary" traits in the person
which do not belong to the definite set called father-complex. But,
when the astrologer speaks of Saturn he means a principle of
activity or quality of being which is found in everything. Everything includes some Saturnian activity; every birth chart contains
all planets, all zodiacal signs, all houses. Everything is in everything. The characteristics of every level can be found in the corresponding sub-levels of every level. Nothing can be excluded
from anything; no feature can be eliminated from any organic
whole as non-characteristic.

This means that if we speak of a father-complex we cannot say
astrologically that it is a Saturn-category, or even that it can be
described by the relation of Saturn to the Moon alone, everything
else being ignored—just as the scientific psychologist purposely
ignores every other feature in the total life of an individual when
he says that this individual suffers from a father-complex. Indeed,
there is or should be no such thing for the astrologer as a "father-
complex" in general; for, to him, the birth chart as a whole
represents the individual person as a whole, and what the psychologist calls father-complex (by isolating a number of characteristic psychological features) has roots and ramifications in every
factor of the birth chart. The astrologer sees, or should see, in
the chart the symbolic representation of a whole person who is *both*
healthy and sick, strong and weak, etc.; while the psychiatrist
deals primarily with a disease which he seeks to cure—a disease
which is a category of specific phenomena, and in many respects
an entity.

Saturn, in any sound astrology, is *not* an entity. It is a quality
or principle inherent in all things whatsoever. And when we defined four basic functions in all organisms, we referred to types of
activities found wherever there is life. To speak of functional
disturbance is not the same as defining a disease as an entity (or
exclusive class of phenomena) with a name; for this disturbance,
if it is truly "functional" implies the entire bio-psychological or
psychosomatic organism or personality—an individual organism

and a *unique case*. Each astrological chart is a unique case. Every moment is unique. The entire celestial pattern of any chart cannot be duplicated in billions of years. No human complex can be exactly duplicated, for it is the production of a whole individual; all his functions contribute to it or to its disappearance. A complex is the entire individual person operating rigidly and under stress in one direction.

All of which is simply to show that it would be quite futile to pin down a complex to a particular astrological situation and to none other. What has to be understood, rather, is that, where a father- and mother-complex exists, its nature can be interpreted and traced back to its source by considering the astrological symbols of the corresponding function, Saturn and the Moon. But one cannot say a priori that a square of Saturn to the Moon, or any particular position of either planet will "cause" a complex. Indeed, no particular astrological factor "causes" any particular condition. It points to the source of the condition when the condition exists; and it only indicates the function and the department of life, experience and personality where it would show up, *if* it shows up at all.

Rather, therefore, than list what might more likely than not (the famous deviation from a statistical average!) be considered to indicate the presence of complexes in a birth chart, we will see how some rather characteristic types of complexes register in the charts of individuals known to have had such complexes. And at the outset we shall emphasize again that where there is a father-complex, there is also a mother-complex of some sort, and that a complex can be produced as well by congestion (too much functioning) as by undernourishment and depletion of the organs or psychic centers responsible for the function.

As an example, let us consider the famous French poet, novelist and statesman, Victor Hugo. Victor Hugo is a typical illustration of the Romantic personality with its emotional intensity, its rebelliousness against authority and formalism, its spiritual yearnings and its social humanitarianism; and he is one of the most constructive and steady, noble and creative manifestations of the type. In other words, he illustrates the positive type of parental complex, the complex used by the individual spirit (and also by the "spirit of the times") for creative ends.

Because of this positiveness, we find that the Sagittarian Moon is in not a too stressful position, being in square to its Nodes and Mercury in Pisces (conjunct the North Node in the 5th house) but also in trine to a 10th house conjunction of the Part of Fortune, Jupiter and Saturn. Hugo's mother was a royalist Vendean, a strong character, and died when he was nineteen and already recognized as a poet. She had been separated from her husband, a fervent revolutionist, a military man with violent emotions. The child grew therefore in an atmosphere of great political tensions and conflicts, and being close to his mother, was made to consider his father as "a symbol of hated authority."

His urge to become an individual different from all others (Saturn-Moon function) was thus energized by attachment to his mother and resentment against his father—quite a normal pattern, especially for a Romanticist. In his case, however, bondage to the mother was successfully transferred to an inner psycho-spiritual level, perhaps thanks to the mother's early death; that is, it took the form of what Jung has called an anima polarization.

We saw previously that the mother's function is to act as a protector, an intermediary between an alien or inimical outer world and the child, and an exemplar of efficacious adjustment to the demands of this outer world. When the adolescent succeeds in making his own adjustments to an environment he no longer fears, he may nevertheless feel insecure in relation to the inner world of the psyche, and to all the dimly experienced forces and images that crowd his unconscious—especially if he is a sensitive person with windows of consciousness widely open to this unconscious realm. What he sees, what presses against these "windows" that open to the great darkness beyond the lighted realm of the ego-consciousness, may cause fear and insecurity; and it does the more so, the less developed the father function (Saturn) is within the individual. The less developed this father function, the more emphasized is the mother function within, or the depen-

dence upon the physical mother. When the latter no longer dominates, then it is the mother-image within the psyche which re-
ceives the emphasis—the *anima*, the Moon inside of the earth's
orbit, which symbolizes a blending of the images of mother and
ideal woman; thus, the Soul-guide, the Redeeming Woman, the
Inspirer, the *Muse*.

Victor Hugo's 10th house Saturn is retrograde in Virgo 3°49',
near Jupiter also retrograde in Leo 29°59' (conjunct the regal star
Regulus, and the Part of Fortune); and it is in opposition to a
triple conjunction of Venus, Pluto and Sun in Pisces 3° to
7½°—which creates a very striking setting for a father-complex,
with enough positiveness in the social (Jupiter) and creative
(Venus) factors to suggest the possibility of a creative use of the
complex by the individual spirit. The suggestion is further enhanced by a strong Mars trine to an 11th house Uranus (symbol
of social idealism and reforming zeal) and in quintile (72° aspect,
symbol of creativity) to a rising stationary Neptune in Scorpio
(itself in trine to Mercury conjunct the Moon's North Node).
Neptune rising controls the four planets in Pisces and the 5th
house of self-expression. This all adds up to a powerful social-
regenerative and Romantic tendency, with a characteristic artistic
focusing (Sun conjunct an exalted Venus) influenced by a
political-occult ideology (Pluto) and an insistent humanitarian
outlook—the whole combination dominated by a proud Jupiterian
sense of social importance and ambition.

Saturn retrograde is most frequently a symbol of inner uncertainty with regard to the father-image. All retrograde planets
suggest as a rule (with many exceptions!) that the corresponding
biological functions have become compressed or repressed in-
wardly as a result of previous frustrations or external inhibitions.
In Hugo's case, he was separated both physically and emotionally
from his father; and this created a psychic emptiness which had to
be filled. He filled it, partly by his love for his mother and all
women (anima function), and partly by his Jupiterian-Martian
ambition. The latter became colored by the very image of his
physical father, the presence of whom he had lacked for his fully

normal growth. The father was a revolutionist, a captain, an ardent man fighting for a social Cause; and unconsciously Victor Hugo, who had missed a physical father, made himself into a transformed likeness of his father. A conservative while his mother lived, he became (especially after the death of his father, when he was only 26) a revolutionist himself—first, in literature; later in politics. And in both fields he reached fame and honor, even though at the cost of a political exile which lasted nearly twenty years.

Saturn in opposition to the Sun, especially where the parental houses (fourth and tenth) are involved, reveals strain and stress in the Saturn function and thus in the relation to the father. It may mean dependence upon and fear of an autocratic father, or a cold and often critical evaluation of the father's behavior and character, causing or caused by estrangement. In Hugo's chart the opposition-aspect is made more intricate and far-reaching by the involvement with other planets. A natal Jupiter-Saturn conjunction has much to do with the social attitude of the individual, especially where the father's attitude leads to its establishment— for, as I wrote previously, the father is the link between the home and society, thus between the two basic functional realms.

Finally, I should stress the fact that the Saturn-Sun, etc., opposition occurs in the houses which symbolize traditionally the two parents—a fact emphasizing the tendency toward a strong parental complex. Much discussion has been going on among astrologers as to which of the two houses represents which of the two parents. To me, the fourth house parent is the one whose image controls the focus of the inner life, whether it is the mother or the father. The tenth house parent is the one whose image controls the development of the public life. But it is probably far more sensible not to separate the parents or the two houses defined by the meridian axis, and to say that both parents and both houses refer to the basic function determining the roots of individual existence, the Saturn-Moon function. The meridian of any chart establishes the line of power and growth which extends from root to seed; and there can be no individual existence without both an inner and an outer life.

While Victor Hugo's birth chart reveals a powerful stress upon the father-image and the resulting complex (which however he was able to use as a creative force in relation with a transformed and inspirational mother-image), when we consider the birth chart of Adolf Hitler, we find an abnormal emphasis upon a negative mother-image represented by an equally negative Moon, swollen up as it were by a conjunction with Jupiter, near the Moon's South Node.

This Moon-Jupiter conjunction in the third house is the psychological key to Hitler's chart,* as it stands nearly alone in the below-the-earth hemisphere; and as the single factor in the empty half of the zodiac defined by an opposition of a 12th house Uranus and a 6th house Mercury nearly coinciding with the horizon. Marc Jones, who made the most complete study of overall planetary patterns in astrological charts (cf. his book "The Guide to Astrological Interpretations"), named such a basic configuration the "Bucket" type, of which he wrote that it reveals "at its best the real instructor and inspirer of others, and at its worst the agitator and the malcontent."†

The examples which Marc Jones gives, including Napoleon Bonaparte, show only one planet in the position of the "handle"

---

*I consider that Hitler had the last degree of Libra rising, and approximately Leo 8° at the midheaven. I presented long ago my reasons for such an ascendant, a few degrees later than the usually accepted one. The final collapse of Nazidom and Hitler's death during the last days of April, 1945, while Pluto was stationary on Leo 7°54′, seem to have confirmed my judgment. Hitler was 56 years old April 20, 1945; may have died about the same day. Mussolini was killed (April 28) just after the full Moon (following the new Moon marking F.D. Roosevelt's death).

†In my book *Person-Centered Astrology* (C.S.A. Press, Lakemont, Ga.) I developed further Marc Jones' concepts and renamed most of them, adding several categories. I called the Bucket a "Funnel Pattern." In some cases it can be interpreted also as a "Wedge." What is conveyed by these names is "the idea that the power generated within the grouping of the nine planets is brought to a focus in a thin stream which is released through the narrow opening of the funnel." If one thinks of a wedge then "the power distributed upon the wide surface of the wedge is focused at the sharp end" (cf. p. 197 and 199).

of the Bucket pattern; but Hitler's Moon-Jupiter conjunction is close enough (Moon in 6°38', Jupiter in 8°15' Capricorn) to lead us to consider the two planets as a unit. As such, it indicates a line of release from the hemispheric concentration of planets above the horizon, which in turn stresses social consciousness and all matters of emotional relationship, especially as the Sun, Mars and Venus retrograde are in Taurus, in the 7th house.

The Moon rules the 9th house which contains two factors of personal strength, the Moon's North Node and the Part of Fortune, the latter in opposition to the Moon-Jupiter pair. And Saturn in Leo is elevated in the 10th house, squaring the exact Mars-Venus conjunction, but in sextile to Uranus, in quintile aspect (72°) to Neptune and Pluto, and in biquintile aspect (144°) to the Moon and Jupiter—the quintile series of aspects referring to what might be called "genius" or at least talent—also in distant trine to Mercury.

What we see thus is a strong Saturn focusing into the tenth house, through a series of aspects, the energies of all the planets near and above the horizon; but the Moon-Jupiter conjunction controlling the below-the-horizon realm (the private life) stubbornly stands. Saturn and the Moon are thus protagonists in a strange psychological drama. They are related through a biquintile aspect; an aspect of dubious psychological meaning which could be said to refer to the reactionary backwash of previous manifestations of creative genius. And here let me stress that there can be "genius" in destruction as well as in construction—and it is in this direction that we should read Hitler's chart.

I am not concerned, however, in this analysis with the ultimate fate of the late Fuehrer of a Germany led to a collective neurosis by the defeat and post-war chaos that followed the Versailles Treaty. I am dealing only with his parental complexes, which in turn provided the dynamic energy necessary for his violent and ruthless public rise. I see the father-image (Saturn) dominating his public life; then an overexpansive mother-image (made receptive by the proximity of the South Node) forcing relentlessly the inner life into a condition of dependence to a peculiar Jupiter-function. I see a birth chart with the last degree of Libra rising, thus ruled by a Taurean Venus which is both retrograde and exactly conjunct Mars, ruler of the 6th and 7th houses. And in this last-mentioned configuration (squared by Saturn) I see the shadow of emotional negativeness, of complete selfishness, and the suggestion that here we may well face a psyche controlled by some collective social power, or worse. Anyone acquainted with the facts of Hitler's youth, and with his chaotic relationship to his parents should realize the actual conditioning to which he was subjected in his childhood.

Consider now the case of the Duke of Windsor, whose unusual destiny, his marriage, and what is generally known of his psychological reactions, unavoidably suggests a strong mother-complex. Here we find the Moon rising in Pisces 3°58' in distant square to a conjunction of Jupiter and Neptune in the 4th house (Gemini), and in exact square to the cusp of this house. Mars is in the first degree of Aries—symbolizing the earliest stage of emergence from the sea of the collective unconscious—in square to a Cancer Sun. Moreover, Saturn and Uranus are both retrograde, and co-rulers of the Aquarian Ascendant; thus we find again retrograde conditions being emphasized with regard to Saturn and the chart's "ruler."

This factor of planetary retrogradation should, it is true, not be thought of as a certain symbol of complexes; yet it does signify a trend which usually is found inevitably associated with the growth of complexes. In the case of Oscar Wilde—a typical instance of fateful mother-complex—we find also the ruler of the birth chart, Mercury, retrograde (in Libra and near the Sun); while a ninth House Taurean Moon is located between Pluto and Uranus retrograde. Saturn is direct, but weak in Cancer (the sign of its detriment or debility) and squaring the Sun. And whoever knows about the elder Wilde and his home can trace easily the factual conditions under which his gifted son developed the paternal complexes which led him to fame—and to imprisonment.

V

The Jupiter-Mercury Function
and its Problems

IN THE preceding chapters I have defined the meaning of the four basic functions, needs, urges or drives upon which the many processes of organic living rest: the urge to be a particular being, the urge to sustain against all disrupting influences the characteristic form or temperament of this particular being, the urge to reproduce it, the urge to transform it according to some kind of purpose. These basic functions are to be found in every living organism at the level of unconscious and compulsive instinct. In the fully developed human person of our epoch, they operate not only at the biological and instinctual level, but more significantly still at the psychological level where they constitute the primary substance of personal feelings and thoughts, where also they condition the responses of the individual to his life-experience, his environment (inner as well as outer) and to the social-cultural patterns or traditions in the midst of which he grows into more or less advanced maturity.

No psychology makes sense which does not recognize the essential interdependence between the psychological and the biological realms of expression of these basic functions. The great trouble with so-called classical or academic psychology is that when it speaks of will, thought, attention, love and hate it deals with abstract entities which are not seen as related to the basic functions of the human organism. The true organism of a man, however, is both physical and psychological; and the same functions operate at both levels, in different ways, yet in interconnected ways. Man's personality is an organic whole, a "psycho-

44

somatic" whole—that is, psyche and body *(soma)* as two interdependent and interacting expressions of the one basic life-power
differentiated into four primary urges or functions.

It may be well to stress here that none of these functions in
man is in itself "spiritual" or "material." They are manifestations
of life. The spirit in man can use these functions and thus invest
them with a spiritual character and purpose; or else they may be
used against the purpose of the spirit (i.e. of human and individual evolution), in which case they acquire a spiritually destructive or frustrating character, even if this use is conducive to so-
called success and prosperity.

This is an important point, as there has been among astrologers
the unfortunate tendency to think of planets as good or evil;
whereas every planet, as symbol of a basic functional activity of
the human personality, can be interpreted as being either constructive and destructive according to the type of use to which the
function is put. The "urge to be a particular being," which we
have seen to be related to the Saturn-Moon pair, is neither good
nor bad in itself. It simply *is*. Yet, if it is used to the point at
which the individual stands utterly isolated and insulated against
all other individuals, then it is an evil force, which in turn poisons
the other functions—particularly the Jupiter-Mercury function
which is closely associated with it. Jupiter, worshipped by
medieval astrologers as the Great Benefic, will also in such a
case become a power for evil. It can of itself be a force of self-
destruction, if the function of self-preservation and self-
sustainment turns into an uncontrolled desire for self-
aggrandizement at any cost.

As we study this second of the four basic life-functions we
should first realize—if we are to understand well the various
types of complexes to which it can give rise when frustrated or
distorted—that it operates in many and varied directions. In one
sense Jupiter is a symbol of health and sanity, of inner integration
and successful living. It makes the life whole and counterbalances
the over-individualistic and separative trend of the ego and its
tool, the analytical mind. But man cannot be truly whole by

living alone in the world. No organism can be healthy without a
constant ebb and flow of exchange with the entities and substances surrounding it. Life implies interchange; thus, in the
broadest sense of the term, commerce—and all forms of commerce and commingling are represented in astrology by Mercury,
the servant (or *shakti*) of Jupiter-Zeus. Jupiter and Mercury are
the two poles of one single basic organic function; and the interplay between these two poles constitutes one of the most profound subjects for study, in astrology and in psychology. This
interplay refers to the fact, stressed by modern psychologists, that
any true psychology of *personal integration* must go hand in
hand with a psychology of *social adaptation.* Health is bound to
"commerce" at all levels. Sanity implies a sound sense of social
relationship.

The Jupiter function is so involved in social participation that
Jupiter can be interpreted as the basic social function. It expresses
the ineradicable need there is for any man to feel himself associated, and to act in effective and harmonic association, with his
fellow men—and as well with all living organisms around him.
Saturn, at the level of social activity, defines, consolidates and
precisely establishes the individual's participation in the life of his
environment and his society; but Saturn, in this sense, must act
upon what Jupiter at first makes real as a feeling of participation
with, and of dependence upon, the environment. There is dependence because any organism must breathe and assimilate food in
order to maintain itself. Jupiter, the sustainer of individual being,
rules therefore over all aspects of the function of *assimilation.*

In order to make clear the relationship between Jupiter and
Saturn we have to see these planets operating at several levels.
Saturn, as symbol (together with the Moon) of the roots of individualized existence, comes first as establishing the primary structural character of the individual organism—its skeleton, then the
rudiments of the ego—before any really social contact is experienced. Then, as the child finds himself related to the external
world, the Jupiter function of social adaptation and participation
develops, which in turn leads to a further consolidation of the ego

(and of the skeleton) around the theoretical "seventh year" (growth of permanent teeth).

We should not forget, however, that before the earliest rudiments of skeleton and organic individuality took form in the mother's womb and in the act of the "first breath," the Jupiter function was already active in the prenatal development of the embryo, through the assimilation of maternal substance. Thus the process of life can be seen as a constant oscillation between the Jupiter and the Saturn polarities, leading from level to level of organic and personal development.

In order to be whole, man, whether as a mere body or as a complex psychosomatic personality, must assimilate products from his biological, psychological, social-cultural (and eventually "spiritual") environment. But assimilation, if it is to be a steady, reliable and expanding operation, implies participation and a give-and-take process. At the earliest historical level, it means not only the gathering of fruits and hunting, but the cultivation of plants and the breeding of animals. At more developed social levels, it means that personal growth implies human interchange, commerce, discussion of ideas and the sharing of spiritual values—including the form of sharing called "sacrifice."

Assimilative processes of themselves are Jupiterian; but, if the Mercurian function of interchange and the sense of mutuality or sharing do not operate in the closest manner with these Jupiterian processes, negative or evil results follow. They follow, for the same reasons that parental complexes are formed which poison or construct the personality if either the Saturn or the Moon function overdevelops at the expense of its polar opposite. If, symbolically speaking, Jupiter overpowers Mercury, or vice versa, new types of complexes are bound to appear: complexes which can affect both the psychological and the physiological health of the individual person. They belong essentially to two categories: one which deals with selfhood and assimilation, the other with participation and sharing.

The Jupiter-Mercury function deals, we said, with the urge to sustain in health and sanity the characteristic form and tem-

48 AN ASTROLOGICAL STUDY

perament of the individual psychosomatic organism. If, however, the Saturn-Moon function defining originally this form of individual being has operated weakly, a situation is created in which, either the Jupiterian power of sustainment, finding nothing very definite to sustain, loses interest (as it were) in a seemingly hopeless task, and seeks a compensatory field of activity in a transcendent realm—or else, this Jupiterian function, challenged by the Saturnian deficiency, strains itself insistently and aggressively, dominating the field of personality.

In the first case, we see developing some kind of deep and poignant *religious sense*. The individual whose structural outlines are as yet indefinite, or are blurred through hereditary weakness and perhaps disease, feels instinctively (and, in time, consciously and perhaps tragically) that he can only sustain his individuality by attaching it to a greater unit of being, within which he may be more secure, and from which he can draw strength by osmosis, as an embryo draws sustenance from the mother's body. In other words, the person born structurally weak (in body or in rudiments of ego) seeks a new and transcendent "mother." The Jupiter function is dedicated to such a quest, which may take a great variety of forms. The primary attitude is always rooted in a realization of structural weakness and thus in a more or less intense or desperate attempt to find encouragement and protection, either from a transcendent "father" or an enfolding supernal "mother," Church or Party. This may be called the feudal attitude, based on complete personal allegiance to a "strong man" (socially or spiritually strong), or to a fraternal or mystical organization.

In the second case above mentioned, the Jupiter function is aroused to determined action and tries strenuously to mask and compensate for the Saturnian inefficiency. This can be done in a number of ways, depending on the family and social environment and its characteristic pressures or challenges. It is done always by a close cooperation between the Jupiter and Mercury poles of the function. Jupiter, generally speaking, builds up *personal glamor* through a keen and avid assimilation of whatever can cover up and disguise the weak points in the Saturnian armor; while Mercury produces *intellectual cunning and sophistry* in order to turn any environmental setup to the individual's advantage.

In these two basic cases the Jupiter-Mercury function is put under abnormal pressure and compelled to operate under strain. A primary sense of inferiority is met in two opposite ways; and either way can lead to the development of strong complexes. The second way is, on the surface, more positive than the first; yet essentially both attitudes are rooted in fear. The feeling of inferiority may produce, by reaction, an aggressive superiority complex (especially if the Mars function is strongly aroused); and this may lead to great personal achievements.

Here, however, we are concerned primarily with the mechanics of operation through which one type of functional deficiency leads to the strained intensification of another function. The word to stress is "strained"; for *any persistent strain leads sooner or later to rigidity*—thus to stiffening, crystallization and ankylosis, auto-intoxication, and psychological complexes stopping the flow of the spirit. The free creativeness of spirit is replaced by the sharpness and ingenuity of mind. The ego weakened by parental complexes is bolstered up by intellectual cunning and sophistry, by mental brilliancy and clever rationalization. What seems to be a strong and aggressive ego is actually a weak sense of individual identity carefully concealed under an overactive and tyrannical Jupiter-Mercury setup, with the accent either on the Mercury-mind or on the social ability to manage people through the deliberate use of personal charm and glamor (with Venus' help), or through intimidation (with Mars' help).

Where the Jupiter-Mercury function does not try to compensate at the social-environmental level for a sense of structural inferiority, physiological or psychological, but instead transforms itself into devotion for the greater self or group able to provide protection and a new incentive to life, Jupiter is usually the dominant pole. Then the Jupiterian function glorifies itself as the "Soul" and rationalizes (with Mercury's help) its position of supremacy over the weak Saturn by philosophizing on the evils of egoism and the need for self-surrender to God or the Church. Hindu culture offers a remarkable example of this psychological play of forces, especially during the Middle Ages which saw an incredible display of devotional self-surrender and utter emotional subservience to the Spiritual Guide *(guru)*. The Hindu *bhakta* (devotee) considers himself the "slave" of his "Master," and places his entire psychic energy at the service of the exalted being who has become father and mother in one. The Saturn-Moon function abdicates completely. The Jupiter function is exalted to the state of godhead. Even Mercury, as mind, is regarded with complete disfavor, except insofar as it serves the dictates of the Jupiter function.

Historically speaking, the entire spiritual revolution which began during the first century B.C.—in India through Northern Buddhism (Mahayana School) and in the Mediterranean world through popular Christianity (especially via St. Paul)—represents a collective psychological reaction in which the Jupiter function received the main "life-accent" after a period of emphasis of the trend toward ego-development. The latter had begun in the West around the time of the Egyptian reformer, Akh-na-ton, (1360 B.C.) and of Moses—the middle of the so-called "Arian" Age. The stress had been put, in one way or another, upon the Saturn function—whether as the disc of the Sun in Egypt, or as Jehovah-Saturn with the Hebrews.

With the Greeks, we find Mercury-intellect developing as the servant of Saturn, and as a result the emphasis was placed upon rationalism and logic—and also, at first, upon *Moira*, Fate or Karma (a Saturnian factor). Later, Greek mythology reveals an attempt to strengthen the Jupiter against the Saturn function, with a corresponding growth of a new social sense and of a feeling of universalism in social organization. Western man, through such collective efforts, accomplished a tentative transition from one level of activity to another; yet failed. The Greek social sense led to anarchy; the Greek intellectuality to sophistry and formalism in thought. And the reaction came in a repolarization of the Jupiter function following the collapse of Greek individualism.

Christianity, in a chaotic and disintegrating Mediterranean world (but temporarily given a semblance of integration by the original Fascism of the Roman Empire) compensated for the debacle of Saturnian individualism by transforming the Jupiter function into a devotional and religious force. The Piscean Age had begun, theoretically ruled by a Jupiter overshadowed by a mystic Neptune (one of the two poles of the "transforming function" which constitutes the fourth of the basic life-functions, according to our classification).

The original Jupiterian Christianity of the Gospel was based on Jesus' injunction to heal men and nations. But by bringing to the fore the Jewish feeling of sinfulness and guilt, the yearning for redemption through sacrifice, and all the old Jewish complexes based on a chaotic sense of ego and inferiority (parental Saturn-Moon complexes), Paul deviated the positive Christ-impulse into channels of psychological escape and emotional devotionalism.

The early Apostles had received, at the Pentecost, the gifts of healing and of speech in all tongues; they had been made healers of a universal community. The Apostolic Brotherhood was not a Mother-Church, but a company of consecrated men. They did not preach a "religion" but a way of transfiguration, leading to the *new Selfhood*—the Jupiterian self transformed by the fire and leaven of the Uranus-Neptune function. The Christianity of Paul and of most of the Church Fathers, on the other hand, was a Jupiterian compensation for a Saturnian function thwarted by the sense of guilt, of sinfulness and remorse which has plagued men since they strove to overcome the pull of the earth-conditioned, tribalistic way of life and to repolarize their consciousness at the level of spirit-conditioned mental activity.

At this new level the Jupiter-Mercury function can operate without straining *spiritually*, instead of *religiously* as a psychological compensation for parental complexes. At this level also it can express itself socially in terms of a new type of relationship which constitutes real democracy—not to be confused with the merely political forms of parliamentarism, which were often inspired by an emotional collective reaction against the tyranny of the European Church and State. But before we come to study the social aspects of the Jupiter-Mercury function, we should consider its operation in terms of the process of "assimilation" which is essential to life.

The central organ of assimilation in the human body is the liver, over which Jupiter rules in astrology. For ages, wise men have said that man's soul resides in the liver; and priests have sought to read omens by studying the patterns revealed by cutting the liver of a sacrificed animal. These beliefs, very strange to modern minds, are rooted in the fact that no organism can sustain itself without absorbing chemical substances from its environment, and transforming these substances so as to make them its own—i.e. similar to its own substance (as-similation). This organic power of chemical transformation is not limited to the liver, but extends to various endocrine glands; however, being a very conspicuous organ (and probably for deeper reasons), the liver has been considered the controlling factor in the process of assimilation.

While the Saturnian ego *differentiates* the common generic life of man into individuality, the Jupiterian soul *synthesizes* individualized expressions of life into the common substance for man's life. At the level of the body, Jupiter (as liver) deals with foodstuffs; at the level of the feelings and mind, Jupiter (as Soul) deals with the various products of social-collective living which constitutes "culture." A culture is the synthesized mass of contributions made by many individual minds to their society, once these contributions have been blended, absorbed and assimilated by the new generations. Culture is like food in the digestive organs of the collective mentality and psyche of a people; and it is the Jupiter function's task, within a particular personality, to do the assimilating.

Mercury operates in adjunction as the factor of collective memory, as the recorder of tradition, as the distributor of energy-impulses regulating the process of psychosomatic assimilation. In the body, it is the nervous system; in the psyche, the capacity to associate images, symbols and concepts which serve to relate new cultural data to a central stream of civilization, a web of primordial ideas characterizing the particular culture as a collective ideological whole. Where the Mercury function fails to do its work, or where the absorbing hunger of Jupiter overwhelms it, various kinds of unbalances develop. The body becomes fat. The mind fills up with unused data and unrelated information.

The inordinate craving for food, whether physical or intellectual-cultural, constitutes a complex. At the level of purely social activity, it becomes a craving for wealth or power. The passion for self-aggrandizement is a typical expression of an overactive Jupiter function. It can be a compensation for a weak Saturn; but it can also reveal a lack of balance between a tyrannical Jupiter and an ineffective evaluation of one's worth and of one's personal capacity. Assimilation causes, at one level the fat body, at another the scholar loaded with cultural materials yet unable to put them to any creative individual use.

When Mercury acts in a purely passive manner, it only memorizes, under the Jupiterian urge to intellectual aggrandizement; yet, in its more positive and essential nature Mercury is not only the servant of Jupiter, but the symbol of the vast sea of electrical energy which is the substance of all mental activity. As the Moon is the mother-aspect of "life," so Mercury is the mother-aspect of "mind." Organic health at all levels depends always upon the establishment of an effective dynamic and harmonic equilibrium between the two polarities of universal energy.

VI

The Astrological Basis of Social Complexes

THE PRIMARY characteristic of Jupiter is that it presides over all processes of assimilation required for the maintenance of organic life; and we saw that assimilation can be considered not only at the physiological level (where it deals with foodstuffs) but as well at the psychological level, where what is to be assimilated is the culture of the society in which the child and youth grows to maturity. Jupiter symbolizes man's ability to satisfy his hunger for food, physical and mental or emotional. Through assimilation the organism reaches maturity at one or more levels; and only the mature organism shows forth to the full, and is able to maintain in relative security, the individual characteristics which the Saturn function defines and stabilizes increasingly during the process of personal development.

Jupiter is the liver in the body, and the soul-alchemist in the psyche. With him works Mercury, distributor of the electrical energy which not only animates the nervous system, but also provides the substance (mind-stuff) for all mental activities. In its dynamic and positive aspect this mind-stuff is an as yet mysterious power, of which the body's electricity is but one aspect; in its retentive aspect Mercury is the faculty of memory, the ability to accumulate and associate sense-data, images, words and finally concepts.

When, in the Jupiter-Mercury function, Jupiter becomes overactive at the expense of the Mercury polarity, the body or the mind tends to become loaded with unused food turning into psychical or intellectual fat. Mercury then acts merely as the servant or slave of Jupiter, as memorizer and classifier of data. The electrical potential of the body likewise becomes, in the man who lives only to eat, completely occupied by the digestive processes and unavailable for more creative activities.

The Jupiter-Mercury function, however, does not deal only with assimilation and the maintenance of health or organic self-hood. No organism can be healthy without a constant ebb and flow of exchange with the entities and substances surrounding it. Even from the point of view of assimilation alone, an adequate supply of foodstuff (psychological as well as physical) can rarely be assured unless a give-and-take activity is established. In agriculture and cattle-breeding, man gives to nature while taking from it. Industry is profitable and expands only through commerce, and all forms of civilization depend on personal interchanges and on a multiplicity of social processes. Health and sanity are bound to commerce and the commingling of individuals; they require a sound sense of social relationship. Moreover, the development of the social sense—and of the still deeper sense of sharing and compassion—is interwoven with that of personality and "Soul" (in the Jupiterian sense of this term).

In other words, personal integration is largely dependent upon, or at least deeply affected by, the capacity for social adaptation and participation; and it is to Jupiter that the development of the social sense, the sense of give-and-take and of participation in a human, and ultimately a cosmic, environment is related. Disturbance in the Jupiter function can manifest therefore in the great variety of typical social complexes and phobias. As always, the basic cause of these is fear and the feeling that one is a weak force surrounded by overwhelming ones; that one must, either in all cases or in a particular set of circumstances, find oneself "inferior to the occasion."

A person's approach to the solution of his psychological problems in many instances, is based upon the need to overcome an early sense of social inferiority; and I am using here the term "social" to include also the experiences that a child meets in his relationship to his brothers and sisters, and (generally speaking) to his earliest family environment, all of which comes under the symbolism of ᴧe third house. And it is important to realize, in this connectioᴧ that the family constitutes a realm of transition, in which the field of the purely biological-organic functions passes by hardly noticeable stages into that of the typical social functions.

The family is based upon the procreative function and the parents-children relationship. Nevertheless the relationships child-to-child, brother-to-brother, brother-to-sister, children-to-servants, children-to-relatives, etc., contain in germ practically all the kinds of relationships later to be experienced in the wider sphere of society. This is indeed the reason why the family is usually considered as the unit-cell of society. It is a nursery in the social sense, and social functions are gradually developed, theoretically in an atmosphere of protective love, within a root-harmony which partakes still of the deeply instinctive and unconscious power of biological adjustment.

We said "theoretically," because, as the fever of individualization at all cost burns through an entire society, as the sense of any real authority whatsoever and the instinct of organic harmony disappear from both the society at large and its component families, the inevitable result is that children become "individuals" soon after birth (it seems!) and that the theoretically protective nursery is transformed into training grounds for struggling wills-to-power. In such an atmosphere any child ever so little handicapped by some physical or psychical inferiority or oversensitiveness is bound to develop either an inferiority complex or its compensation, an aggressive superiority complex. The precocious and biologically immature individualization of children is the curse of the modern family, and is responsible for endless neuroses; and the cause of it is largely the collective failure of modern parents to assume fully and significantly their vital-spiritual functions as the archetypal Father-Saturn and Mother-Moon—as exemplars of structural-social integration (Saturn) and of the ever-vigilant and ever-effective power of adjustment to everyday situations and needs (Moon).

Because parents are too busy or too careless to demonstrate the authority that comes from practically adequate and soul-satisfying example—the only authority which compels a wholesome acceptance and a healthy devotional response from the child—the modern family moulds precocious and disharmonious, egocentric and complex-ridden individualists who, when grown up, turn society into a battlefield and a jungle. The effect becomes cumulative after a few generations, especially as movies and radios fill the child's impressionable mentality with the very stuff out of which more virulent emotional complexes are made. Social and emotional glamor feeds the growing inferiority complexes. The maudlin sentimentalism or now the eroticism and violence filling so many movies and cheap popular books plus the "Superman" nonsense of cartoons make it almost impossible for children to develop normally and healthily their Mars-Venus function.

The result is that social complexes, which were individual occurences in the vast majority of old-time families, have now reached the collective stage of a permanent "epidemic." Social neuroses are today indeed endemic, i.e. constantly found everywhere in a global world in chaos. It is as a desperate psychological attempt to run away from these social neuroses that men and women have sought the rigid sense of unanimity provided by totalitarian political parties and by old or new, but strongly organized, religions.

The need for authority is gnawing at the confused souls of modern individuals; but the only authority they are offered is that of techniques that supposedly work practical wonders, and of systems (economic, political or religious) made into fanaticism-compelling ideologies or causes. True authority, however, is always *personal*; in the sense that it can only be demonstrated by a peron who acts as a living exemplar and whose actual and individual being *incorporates a solution to the need of those surrounding him.*

As this occurs, this person acquires authority as an agent of the spirit, whose essential character it is to offer creative solutions to all vital needs. He ceases to be an individual person to those who

recognize his spirit-revealing function, and he becomes a Person-
age that is, a man *with* authority—which does not mean *in* official authority! Such a man becomes a social Image after his death
and is likely to give rise to a "myth." These men are the true
Fathers of civilization, the molders of society; and we should add
to them women whose public example makes them Mothers of
civilization and great symbols of personal response to a crucial
need of the times.

The exemplar with authority at the social level focuses in him
the power of the Jupiter function in its highest meaning. He is
"God's agent"—the original High Priest; and in a more individual sense, he is the Hindu *guru*, or spiritual Teacher. He is
also, in a general way, every teacher; for at any level, it is the
function of the teacher to serve as a link between the accumulated
harvest of the human past and the need of the future
generations—just as the parents, in a biological sense, are links
between the hereditary past of the race and the "souls" seeking
experiences and self-focusing in human organisms. The lowered
social standing of teachers in the modern world is another index
to, and cause of, our social chaos.

The preservation of a society and a culture depends upon the
Jupiter-Mercury function, as it is based on religion and education.
The entrance of the power of religion and education into the
biological sphere of the family means an intrusion of society into
the home. When this entrance is of a negative character, the
potential conflict between children and parents, brothers and
brothers, etc., takes on an acute character and leads to the formation of social complexes. These are primarily based on fear, born
of a sense of isolation and inferiority, and secondarily on the
attempt to overcome fear and insecurity through acquisitiveness,
lust, greed, aggressiveness and anger.

I cannot here discuss in detail the extraordinarily varied ways in
which these complexes manifest, from the many phobias to the
multiple forms of sadism and oppression-mania, from avaricious-
ness to the bitterest pangs of envy, from kleptomania to the

aggressiveness of the great conquerors. These are all expressions of a thwarted, frustrated, perverted or exaggerated sense of social relationship. One type of complex, however, should be singled out because it involves not only the social and the religious realms, but reaches down to the very roots of individual existence—the "guilt complex."

The sense of guilt is based on a sense of personal isolation, even though it also fosters this sense of isolation. But it is as well a social-religious (Jupiterian) manifestation, because it is born of a feeling of disharmonious—and ultimately destructive—participation in the group-life. This feeling, in turn, makes the individual turn against and destroy himself subtly or violently. The two planetary functions basically involved are, thus, Jupiter's and Saturn's. Yet because the sense of guilt frustrates or hinders the individual's attempts at self-transformation and at reaching a higher or broader type of participation in the social or universal life, the Neptunian function and the natal house dealing with *personal* crises of growth (the sixth house) should be considered for basic clues.

What people call the voice of conscience is the manifestation of a thwarted function of self-transformation. Any individual should be able to take the next evolutionary step ahead in his personal or group life, yet he is often impelled backward by inertia and by the memory-pull of ancient experiences, whether pleasurable or tragically haunting; thus, the Uranus-Neptune power that would enable him to grow "from worm into butterfly" is frustrated, and in its defeat it hounds the unfortunate human being, reproaching him for his weakness. The result is a sense of guilt, which may be collective as well as individual—the more collective, the stronger the sense of tribal or social participation.

The sense of guilt leads to the craving for redemption; and just as a sense of inferiority may lead to an aggressive feeling of superiority, likewise the yearning for redemption may lead, on its active and forceful side, to a Messiah-complex and a poignant desire to redeem others, and unconsciously to escape the responsibility to transform oneself. However one should speak of a Messiah-complex only if the individual is escaping his responsibility for self-transformation. In the true Redeemer, it is the power of his inner metamorphosis which becomes so intense and radiant as to affect, by spirit-borne contagion, his community and perhaps humanity as a whole. He is a true Redeemer, because the spirit is able *to use his individual redemption* as an example. He acts as a healing force answering the need for redemption of a small or vast group of men. The individual Uranus-Neptune function is thus "hooked up," we might say, to the vast all-human and universal power of revolutionary growth. God transforms humanity *through* the individuals who transform themselves— especially if this individual metamorphosis focuses, in its outstanding character and intensity, the basic need of humanity or of a portion of humanity *at the time*, and thereby gives it a *symbolic and collectively valid meaning.* Every act of God is symbolic and impregnated with a collectively valid meaning.

From the preceding, it should be clear that social-religious complexes can be of so many types as to make their astrological representations equally varied and not to be reduced to a few standardized planetary configurations. In seeking to track down astrological indications which can be regarded as *potential* sources of social-religious complexes, Jupiter, Mercury and Neptune are the main factors to consider; but, as we already saw, these factors must always be studied in relation to the way in which the Saturn-Moon function operates, as social-religious complexes are, in many cases, the results of, and compensations for, an unbalanced or frustrated relationship to the parents. Moreover, much depends upon the contents and rulership of certain natal houses, especially the third and ninth (also upon the Part of Fortune, which is one of the strongest indications of the "social sense"— together with the Parts of Jupiter and Saturn).

These two planets have been called the "planets of the Soul," but obviously all depends upon what one exactly means by this confusing term "soul." According to the way a Jungian psychologist usually understands the word, the soul constitutes the polar opposite of the ego; as Jupiter, the polar opposite of Saturn. However, as the two factors are constantly interwoven and interdependent, it is entirely legitimate to say that the "soul life" is the result of their inter-relatedness. This inter-relatedness finds its essential expression in the Father-image; i.e. in a person's relationship to his father and attitude toward everything that refers psychologically and socially to fatherhood—including particularly all forms of religious and political authority. This is so because, as I already pointed out, the traditional father is both a part of the family circle and the active representative of the family in the outer world of society—and of society in the inner world of family. In him, therefore, the biological and the social spheres, the primordial home and the community-life, interpenetrate.

The distinction between these two spheres, and also between the mother (as symbol of home life) and the father (symbol of public social life), is no longer as sharp as it used to be. Therefore, modern astrology finds it very difficult to say which of the fourth and tenth houses corresponds to the father, and which to the mother. The fourth house is nevertheless the sphere of private and personal (thus, "soul") integration; while the tenth house is that in which the formed individual establishes his place and his function in the universe and in society—and this place is the foundation of the ego. It is ruled by Saturn.

The astrological relationship between Jupiter and Saturn indicates thus the relationship between one's sense of "place" in society and one's sense of personal soul-integration—the latter being fed by the Moon function, but established as a conscious psychological factor by the Jupiter function. When Jupiter forms a square (and semi-square) with Saturn, a state of dynamic tension is shown to exist in the personality. This state can be either destructive or regenerative. It reveals in any case a conflict within the individual between the traditional social sense of "place" and the drive toward inner personal integration. It indicates a strong spiritual dissatisfaction with accepted social and personal standards. The power of this potentially "divine" discontent can lead the individual to a transformation and broadening of his sense of selfhood, as well as of his participation in the world and in society; it may also produce very strong social complexes caused by an endemic state of rebellion against all forms of authority.

On the other hand, a natal conjunction of Jupiter and Saturn indicates the probability of the emergence of a *new* sense of personal or social integration within the individual, a new type of alignment with the universal or social whole (Hermann Keyserling, F. D. Roosevelt, for instance); while the opposition between Jupiter and Saturn reveals a life most likely featuring a deep inner decision (as a rule somewhere during the thirties or forties) or a radical change in external social conditioning which will transform the root-implications of destiny.

What happens essentially in these cases of focalized Jupiter-Saturn relationship is either that the preserving Jupiterian function finds itself altered by a radical transformation in the personal or social structure-conditioning Father-image (Saturn), or that the individual ego (Saturn) is compelled to experience some kind of reconstruction because of the breakdown of the preserving Jupiter function. A religious conversion or a sudden loss of wealth, prestige or health would be possible instances of such a breakdown.

The 20-year transit cycle of the Jupiter-Saturn conjunctions is of capital importance in forecasting potential crises in the social sense of an individual and in his approach to personal integration. The passage of Jupiter over the natal "angles" (ascendant, midheaven, etc.) and through the houses during its approximate 12-year cycle is also of utmost importance; and this transit-cycle has been used extensively in the field of business.

A retrograde Jupiter can be considered a significant indication, provided the astrologer is able to interpret this factor in terms of the entire chart-pattern and does not jump to standardized conclusions. A number of instances of retrograde Jupiter are found in the charts illustrating Marc Jones' book "The Guide to Horoscope Interpretation," and listing them will show at once that no obvious conclusions as to the social or financial meaning of such a natal Jupiter should be reached: Theodore Roosevelt, Cecil Rhodes, Andrew Carnegie, Karl Marx, Prince Bismarck, Lord

Byron, Francisco Franco, Mahatma Gandhi, Goethe, George Washington, Louis Pasteur. A strange collection of powerful and highly significant individuals!

Let us look briefly at a few of these charts. Theodore Roosevelt and Cecil Rhodes (the great British empire-builder and diamond magnate) were both, in their youth, sick. The former has Jupiter retrograde in Gemini and the 6th house; the latter in Sagittarius and the 12th house. By overcoming or using this condition they developed their power. Theodore Roosevelt's Mars rising and culminating Scorpio Sun gave him the necessary drive; and the Mars-Moon opposition on the horizon, plus the perfect Cross made by the Jupiter-Venus opposition squaring Neptune and the Part of Fortune, tell a story of overcoming of a strong mother-complex and regenerative personal will. In Andrew Carnegie's chart Jupiter retrograde stands isolated, squared by Pluto, opposing the Part of Fortune; but the first house Sun-Mars conjunction gives also violent energy. Cecil Rhodes' Part of Fortune is conjunct Jupiter, square Neptune, and opposing Mars. Karl Marx' retrograde Jupiter opposes Mars, but is in sextile to a dominant Saturn-Pluto conjunction; and we find him the builder of a practical technique (sextile) of social rebellion.

The fact that Jupiter is retrograde at birth certainly does not mean that the individual will be a weak or retiring social person, or an introvert. But it does mean usually that this individual will meet problems of self-preservation in his environment— problems which, if overcome, will be the very foundations of his destiny and his strength. These may refer to health, or social status; or they may be focused by social sympathy and indignation at social abuses (as in the case of Gandhi, Marx, et al.). But they are problems causing the individual to question and challenge traditionally and socially accepted values. If the challenge is successful the individual may reach fame or wealth; otherwise he may go down as a criminal or a social wreck. The complex is there in either case.

VII

Mercury Problems

THERE IS much more to Mercury than is usually taught in astrological textbooks. Mercury is said to be the symbol of the
mind; but this term "mind" covers a multitude of mysteries, and
Mercury can be seen to represent a variety of processes and functions in the personality, especially as the latter is developing
beyond the normal range of activities familiar to the average
cultured individual of our day and age.

If we look at the solar system from a heliocentric point of view,
Mercury is seen as the first planet revolving around the sun. It
thus can be said to refer to the primary differentiation of the
undifferentiated solar energy radiating through space. As such
Mercury represents the bi-polar electrical force which is the very
substance of all organic activity. This Mercury-electricity is the
"tone" of life sustaining and ever renewing the organism isolated
by birth as an independently functioning unit, foundation for an
individual personality. This "tone" (individualized Solar power)
is the *involutionary* expression of Mercury, and it is said to be
focused at the center of the cross formed by the human spine and
the line of the extended arms. It represents the power-aspect of
Mercury.

This mystic Mercury center is the "place" where the Rose
blooms at the core of all crucifixions significantly experienced in
the spirit of Christ, according to Rosicrucian symbolism. It corresponds to the brachial plexus of modern anatomy, which is the
very focus of the Mercury function. Traditional astrology attributes to this planet rulership over arms, hands, lungs and breath;

and there seems to be a definite connection between the brachial nerves and the Vagus nerve (pneumogastric system) which originates in the head (Aries rulership) and flows downward in two branches on either side of the neck.

We spoke of this aspect of Mercury as "involutionary" because it refers to the primordial descent and prenatal differentiation of the one Solar power which is the essence of individual life and selfhood. However, what is usually known of the Mercury function is its "evolutionary" aspect which deals with the results of personal and social living; and in this role Mercury is the servant of Jupiter. Mercury then should serve the purpose of personal integration, and of the maintenance and aggrandizement of the wholeness of personality. Mercury in this role is mind, not as a creative electrical power, but as the function of relationship of self to environment and to other selves.

We must differentiate carefully, however, between the type of adaptation to environment which corresponds to the Moon function, and that which carries the characteristics of Mercury. The former is "placental" and psychic; the latter, nervous and mental. The Moon function, being the "feminine" polarity of Saturn, adjusts the personality to its environment within the separative boundaries of the particular body and ego; but it can go no further. It deals with the *tribal* kind of adaptation to life and is inherently conservative, traditional and appropriative or possessive. On the other hand, the Mercury function, being (in its evolutionary and personalized aspect) the feminine polarity of Jupiter, carries the essential meaning of expansion and accretion, as does Jupiter. It brings to the personality a *plus* quality; and therefore it can become the very foundation for the development of the substance of personality from one level to the next.

The power actually to accomplish this transference of consciousness from level to level (or metamorphosis of personality) is contained in the functions of transformation symbolized by the planets beyond Saturn, particularly Uranus; yet the revolutionary and regenerative power of Uranus can only be destructive or useless if the individual has not developed the substantial mental foundation upon which the new-level consciousness and individuality can unfold organically and harmoniously. To move from one level to the next means actually to enlarge one's sphere of awareness, thus one's power to operate in an even more inclusive realm of being. And this can only be done by increasing one's capacity for relationship.

But relationship between what? At first, what is to be related are sensations, then, complex images combining sensations; later, the apparent sources of these images (objects, people, etc.). A further step in relatedness is taken as these sources of complex sensation-images are given the attributes of personality, and thus can be related to one's ego. The sense of ego-to-ego relationship, within some larger environmental and tribal (or family) framework of well-defined and life-sustaining experiences, becomes the substance for social living.

The Jupiterian hunger for food and easier living conditions stimulates inevitably this sense of relatedness to external entities, to which at first the attributes of personality are given, whether they be rocks, trees, animals or human beings. Primitive life is difficult; the environment full of dangers and antagonisms. The Jupiter function demands that a way be found to make friends with and influence everything in the environment. Tribal magic, prayers, sacrifices and all the instrumentalities of the religious life are developed through a combination of Jupiterian faith in some underlying universal harmony (without which no man could come to terms with other men, gods or life-spirits), and of Mercurian ingenuity in building bridges of communication and means of commerce through give-and-take operations pleasing all parties concerned. The use of imitative vocal sounds, soon becoming words and taking form as letters and art-symbols, then the use of objects of standardized values as means of exchange (money and all its cultural equivalents) constitutes the basic ways in which Mercury operates, as social experiences grow in complexity and scope.

Inventiveness (born of the faculty to see correlations between facts and phenomena of different kinds), conceptual generalization (which transforms the Jupiterian feeling or intuition of universal harmony into the study of cosmic laws), and the ability to "bind time" through historical records and communal education, are the building stones of civilization—and they all are aspects of Mercurian activity. This activity is stirred by the Jupiterian craving for self-preservation and for all types of group-cooperation and group-expansion insuring more comfort and a greater sense of happiness through easier participation in the life rhythms of the universe.

This Mercury activity is so complex, so inclusive, so far reaching that it may normally seek to utilize and control an ever-increasing amount of the energy and power of attention disposable in the personality. But, if it does so at the expense of the polar and complementary Jupiter function, a situation arises in which the means to increase the individual's ability to relate himself to ever larger fields of reality expand at the cost of his power vitally to experience and to assimilate (Jupiter) what he becomes related to. The result is the great disease of modern civilization, from which endless complexes and psychosomatic troubles arise: *intellectual congestion*. It is the disease responsible for the atomic bomb and the ruthless mentality of men who "know too much for their own good" because their intellectual knowledge is no longer balanced by a deep and intense sense of participation in the whole life of society and the universe. In these men, intellect—which should be only a sum-total of means—has become a devouring power blinding them to the essential end of human existence, immortality in conscious selfhood. Jupiter, the planet of Soul, has been overcome by its mate and natural servant, Mercury, the planet of technique and efficiency.

The generalized development of the modern intellect, based on Saturnian logic and thus deeply allied with a parallel process of ego-emphasis, can be said to have begun in Greece—though India also experienced the results of overrationalization and of a special type of spiritual selfishness. It led in Greece to sophistry and an orgy of argumentative speculations, and much of it recurred within a new framework during the Scholastic Age in Europe.

With the advent of modern experimental science and of mechanistic-intellectual theories of knowledge, the emphasis became placed upon the technical aspect of the Mercury function and upon a worship of intellectual curiosity, unbalanced by any realization of the fact that to know without the knowledge of *what one knows for* can be a slow form of suicide. Technical proficiency without the ability to place it at the service of a spiritually valid purpose, or as an escape from facing the need to develop a more effective and less egocentric feeling of participation in humanity, is likewise bound to lead to spiritual selfishness and pride, and perhaps eventually to some kind of moral self-destruction.

Any individual today living, and with a normal amount of Western education and mental training, is faced with the possibility of succumbing to this contagious disease of intellectualism and "knowledgitis," with its by-products of sterile overspecialization and atrophy of the sense of direct and vitally experienced living. However, focalized expressions of this generalized functional unbalance appear only in the lives of individuals who offer a fertile psychological soil for its development; and when this occurs we should look for indications of the condition in everything concerning the natal Mercury.

A whole book might be written studying various approaches to the interpretation of this planet in nativities; here, however, we must limit ourselves to a consideration of what is probably the basic issue where Mercury is concerned: Mercury's relationship to the Sun and the Moon. Psychologically speaking, what is at stake is the particular way in which the individual's mind operates with reference to the bi-polar life-principle represented by the two "Lights."

A deep rivalry can exist between the realms of mind and of organic vitality; this rivalry often tears modern man apart. Conscious thought challenges the rule of unconscious instinct, when man seeks to transfer the focus of his being from the bio-psychic tribal level to that of individual differentiation and self-determination through thought. Reason opposes feeling; adaptation in terms of the generic purpose of biological and psychic survival is frustrated and opposed by man's new determination to meet his experiences as a conscious thinker and a "free" individual and to forego mortal well-being for an immortal selfhood established in mind.

It is this conflict which basically produces intellectual complexes—either because, try as he may, the individual feels unable to marshal enough mental power to re-focus his individuality from the realm of "life" to that of "mind," or because, spurred on by an overeager and ambitious mentality, he unwillingly loses his sense of rootedness in bio-psychic desires and vitality, though he can as yet not let go of their instinctual pull, which in such circumstances takes on a "fateful" character. In either case he finds himself in between two realms, unrooted and unfocused. In the first instance, instinctual living at the bio-psychic level of vital feelings and desires has lost its value, yet the mind is too weak, too uncertain or too confused to carry the burden of complete and integral reality. In the second instance, the mind is strong, restless, or overstimulated by external influences or various psychological pressures (mainly by some kind of father-complex), but the rest of the personality, clinging to the old desire for life-fulfillment and generic happiness, cannot or refuses to follow the mind.

Indications of such conditions in the natal chart can be of various kinds, depending upon the manner in which these psychological conditions arise during the early development of the personality; yet some important phases of the relationship of Mercury to the Sun and the Moon should always be studied, along the following lines of enquiry.

The most obvious, yet often misinterpreted factor is whether Mercury is "direct" or "retrograde" in its motion. What this actually means, let us not forget, is whether Mercury moves *in the direction of the motion of Sun and Moon, or against it.* Planetary retrogression is caused by the fact that the observer on earth gets, as it were, a biased or twisted view of the solar system, of which the earth is a part. No one can evaluate with absolute objectivity that in the midst of which one operates. Earthly man's direct evaluation of planetary behavior is thus, partly at least, subjective—that is, biased by referring the behavior of the other planets of the solar system to his own geocentric position. This is so particularly in the cases of Mercury and Venus, because these planets are moving within the Earth's orbit.

Mercury, the mind, operates within the human personality. It operates in close proximity to the very source of life in man, the Sun. About three times every year (that is, on the background of a complete solar cycle) Mercury oscillates to and fro around the Sun—thus making six geocentric conjunctions. Three times Mercury passes between the Earth and the Sun (inferior conjunctions); three times it moves beyond the Sun (superior conjunctions). Before and after the inferior conjunctions Mercury appears, to the earth-observer, to move backward, thus in a direction opposite to that of the Sun's motion; and at times it appears to stand still or "stationary."

A natal Mercury retrograde does *not* in any way mean a weak, dull, or lazy mind—in spite of many students' idea that this should be the case. It indicates, however, generally speaking, a mind which operates inherently *in counterpoint to the instinctual nature and the flow of the life-force.* This, of itself alone, can indicate a great many things; and it is never wise to jump to conclusions merely because Mercury is retrograde at birth! Benjamin Franklin is said to have had his natal Mercury retrograde, yet he was one of the most outstanding thinkers of his century. John Gadbury, one of the greatest European astrologers, and Abdul Baha, the great Persian Prophet and religious leader, also had Mercury retrograde at birth; and so did countless great men.

The important factor to consider here is the basic relationship established in the personality between, on one hand, the consciousness and its mechanisms of awareness or attention (Mercury), and on the other hand, the vital drives of the organism or the compelling purpose of destiny (Sun). There are for man stages of spiritual evolution at which the greatest growth is accomplished through *contrasting* pulls between the Mercury and Sun factors in personality—and this may occur at every level of development, in the primitive person (or "young soul") as well as in the highly evolved (culturally or spiritually) person.

OF PSYCHOLOGICAL COMPLEXES

Mercury retrograde simply indicates the presence of such a contrast. It may lead to a greater state of individualization by a revolt of the mental life against the instinctual-generic nature of feelings; or it may lead, at its worst, to a neurotic mentality always at war with life, building one fancied self-delusion after another in terms of psychological escape from actual facts. It may mean a lucid mental independence from irrational unconscious energies, or slavery to mental fears and subjective deceptions or rationalizations.

On the other hand, a direct Mercury may mean a mentality conditioned primarily by the need for organic survival and personal expansion (from primitive cunning, to a scientific intellect discovering new relations and new tools for the sake of gain and increase in power), or a mind able to give objectivity and effective formulation to the central Solar will and purpose of the individual.

These mental characteristics (or polarizations) are rarely permanent throughout a life, even if a basic tendency can be detected. And here is where the "progressions" of Mercury throughout the years of a life help us to complete the picture. The retrograde periods of Mercury last about 20 to 25 days; thus, by progression (one day after birth equaling one year of the life), the same number of years. If this retrograde period falls within the span of the individual's life-progressions, a definite change in the conscious attitude of the mind is to be expected during the year when the "progressed Mercury" is stationary (thus changes from "direct" to "retrograde" or vice versa), whether or not the change is emphasized by external events.*

The distinction between a direct and retrograde Mercury is not, however, the only one to express the inherent dualism (or bipolar nature) of the mind. Traditional in astrology is the differentiation between a Mercury which rises before the Sun at dawn,

---

*These changes in motion of the progressed Mercury are as valid when calculated by "converse progressions," that is when one day *before* birth (starting from the exact birth-time) is made to represent one year of the life.

In this case the "change of mind" can be seen as due to fateful (or Karmic) pressure rooted in an ancient racial or spiritual past.

and Mercury rising after the Sun. In the first case, Mercury's longitude in the zodiac is less than that of the Sun, and Mercury is a "morning star"; in the second case, it is greater, and Mercury is an "evening star."

The same dualism of position with reference to the rising or setting Sun has been used even more widely where Venus is concerned; and logically it should have a similar meaning in the case of both of these "inner" planets—that is, of planets moving within the Earth's orbit and in close zodiacal proximity to the Sun. As Morning Star, Venus was called "Lucifer", meaning the Bearer of Light. As Evening Star, Venus was named "Hesperus", meaning "in the West." As morning stars Venus or Mercury can be said to be symbolical heralds of the Sun. At or near their maximum distance in longitude from the Sun (28 degrees for Mercury, 47 degrees for Venus) they shine clearly in the sky; when close to their conjunction to the Sun, they (especially Mercury) are lost in the "aura" of light of the Sun.

Marc Jones has based a classification of mental temperaments on whether the natal Mercury is a morning or evening star (cf. "How to Learn Astrology"). Mercury, as morning star, he writes, indicates a mind that is "eager"; and when more than 14 degrees away from the Sun, a mind "not only eager but also untrammeled." Mercury as evening star is said to point to a mind that is "deliberate" or careful, and when more than 14 degrees from the Sun, deliberate and also untrammeled—that is, independent from the Solar will or self.

This Mercury dualism of position is said further to correlate with the fact that "the only important difference between one mind and another is the underlying or general tendency of one individual to reach forward and anticipate things, and of another to lean back and recapitulate them, together with the further distinction by which some minds do this in a rather extreme degree, whereas others remain relatively close to the central balance of will." This dualism was also known to the ancient philosophers under the symbolism of the two mythological figures of Prometheus and Epimetheus, prototypes of the "progressive" and the "conservative," of him who seeks to focus ahead of time the radiance of tomorrow (the Prophet), and of him who gathers to himself the light of the past (or "who takes counsel after the event"). Indeed, just as the Venus function can be known under two aspects as Lucifer and Hesperus, so the Mercury function can operate according to two basic rhythms in relation to the spirit-source within man, as Prometheus and Epimetheus.

Marc Jones is no doubt right on the whole in characterizing the Promethean mind as "eager," and the Epimethean mind as "deliberate"; but underneath this distinction a still more basic one can be discovered. The Promethean mind is one in which the involutionary, electrical and creative aspect of the Mercury function is eminently active; while in the Epimethean mind it is the evolutionary, associative, recapitulative and generalizing aspect of Mercury which predominates.

However, if we accept this classification of the two basic aspects of the Mercury function (that is, of Mercury *geocentrically* considered), our interpretation of retrograde Mercury must be qualified by it. When Mercury emerges from its inferior conjunction with the Sun in a retrograde direction, it becomes and remains a morning star. The "eager" Promethean Mercury-mind can also be *at the same time* a "retrograde" Mercury; and after its superior conjunction with the Sun Mercury is both Epimethean and "direct." .

A significant and logical solution to the problem this poses can be found by considering the cycle of Mercury's motion from the *heliocentric* point of view and in its relation to the successive heliocentric conjunctions and oppositions of the Earth and Mercury. Mercury is essentially a "solar" planet; and likewise "mind" is, of itself, an expression of being closer to the spirit than to the earthly nature of man. What is at the root of all mental problems is the basic adjustment of spirit (Sun), mind (Mercury) and body (Earth) in a total personality. The study of such an adjustment is the most valid key to the "chemistry of the mind," and thus to the foundation upon which abnormal or disharmonious manifestations of the Mercury function can be expected to arise under various kinds of stimuli.

VIII

The Cycle of Mercury and the Functioning of the Mind

IN THE usual kind of geocentric astrology no distinction is made between the two kinds of conjunction of Mercury and the Sun, except that at "inferior" conjunction Mercury is retrograde, while at "superior" conjunction Mercury is direct. In heliocentric astrology the situation is quite different, because an inferior geocentric conjunction of Mercury and the Sun means that the Earth is *conjunct* Mercury, while a superior geocentric conjunction indicates that the Earth is in *opposition* to Mercury. Thus when Mercury is retrograde geocentrically, Mercury is heliocentrically near the Earth; and at the heliocentric conjunction of Mercury and the earth, a line is formed by Sun, Mercury and Earth, with Mercury and Earth, with Mercury between the Sun and the Earth—thus as near to the Earth as it can ever be.

The situation at such a heliocentric conjunction of Mercury and the Earth (i.e. Mercury retrograde in inferior conjunction to the Sun, in geocentric astrology) is thus analogical to that met at the new Moon, when the Moon passes between the Earth and the Sun, thus is in geocentric conjunction with the Sun. Such a Sun-Moon conjunction is taken to be the beginning of the "lunation cycle." At that time, symbolically speaking, the lunar agencies, whose task it is to build life-organisms, are fecundated and given direction by the Sun; the will and purpose of the Sun is impressed upon them, and this impression is like the impact of a sound shaping loose sand into vibratory patterns, or like the effect of a magnet upon iron-filings.

The heliocentric conjunction of Mercury and Earth means very much the same thing in the realm of mind. The Solar will (or energy-potential) flows outward to the Earth and human beings through the channel of Mercury; the latter differentiating it into that electrical power which is the occult essence of mind (considered as "creative power" and not as "associative memory"). This marks the beginning of a new cycle of relationship between Earth and Mercury—a cycle thus measured by the distance between two successive *inferior* conjunctions of Mercury and Sun in geocentric astrology.

This cyclic fecundation of the Mercury-mind by the Solar energy-potential and purpose occurs about every one hundred sixteen days or every four months, thus three times a year. It occurs when Mercury is retrograde; and this obviously throws a new and at first surprising light on the meaning of the retrograde phase of Mercury. Why does Mercury move, *from the point of view of man on the Earth,* against the direction of the Sun just when it is transmitting in a most focalized manner the Solar potential of energy to the Earth?

This apparent paradox can be understood when one realizes that the emergence of strong and focalized mental activity in man means actually a more or less clear-cut rebellion against the dictates of life-instincts and the irrationality of bio-psychic images or idols. Prometheus is pictured as a rebel, and so are in Hindu mythology the cosmic Intelligences (Manasaputras) who gave to men the "fire of mind" and thus made them *potential gods.* To ordinary mankind at the *geocentric and egocentric* stage of evolution the Sun is "the great Autocrat of the Universe," the symbol of emotional and emotion-rousing compulsive power. Likewise Leo, the sign of the Sun's maximum intensity, is the sign of dictatorial and dramatic persons, whose generosity is only matched by their absolutism.

Life gives abundantly, but commands ruthlessly. Its gifts are balanced by its compulsions. It exalts only those who obey unquestionably its rule. Only by rebelling against this rule—and against the secondary rule of Jupiterian religious and cultural traditions which likewise *bind while integrating* the personality—can mind impress its character upon Earth-conditioned and biologically or socially controlled man. Thus when man begins to realize what mind is and to transfer his focus of awareness from the realm of bio-psychic instincts to that of clear thinking and creative ideas, this new mental activity must inevitably at first appear to him as the enemy of instinctual life. At least the development of the mind must seem to *run counter* to the natural flow of vitality and even of what, under the Jupiterian rule of religion and the tribal spirit of unanimity, the would-be "free thinker" has been taught to consider God-like.

The development of the mind and of the power to determine one's self and one's individual purpose through clear thinking is at the core of the development of individuality; and as man becomes more and more an "individual" he usually at first sees his vitality impaired. He experiences illness and the psychological curses attached to the Promethean gift. As Mercury-Prometheus bids man to be a thinker and an individual through the use of the Solar fire wrested from heaven, this fire burns and destroys. Though it be one in essence with the very source of all life, mind at first appears to operate against life; thus it is logical indeed to find that Mercury-Prometheus is at first a *retrograde* Mercury.

Later, however, the originally experienced opposition between the direction of "mind" and that of "life" disappears gradually. Mercury becomes "stationary," then "direct"; and it moves not only in the same direction as the Sun, but toward the Sun, geocentrically speaking. It reaches this Sun at its "superior" conjunction, that is when heliocentrically speaking, Mercury is in opposition to the Earth, and the Sun stands between these two planets—just as, at full Moon the Earth stands between the Moon and the Sun. Actually Mercury can be shown to have phases corresponding to those of the Moon. Mercury is "full" at superior conjunction with the Sun—it is also at its greatest distance from the Earth, and it appears of minimum size.

The Promethean character of Mercury begins at inferior conjunction, when Mercury is retrograde, and between the Earth and Sun; its Epimethean character is revealed at superior conjunction when Mercury direct is on the other side of the Sun. Mercury-Prometheus corresponds to the *waxing* half of the lunation cycle, which takes on its character from the New Moon. Mercury-Epimetheus corresponds to the *waning* half.

The following table shows how the dualism of Promethean and Epimethean relates itself to that of retrograde and direct motions, from both the geocentric and the heliocentric points of view. It provides us with the basis for a four-fold classification of human mentality.

Geocentric	Heliocentric	Prometheus-Epimetheus	Retrograde-Direct
"New" Mercury. Inferior conjunction	Mercury conjunct Earth	Promethean phase begins, negative to the Sun	Mercury is retrograde
Waxing Crescent phase some 11 days later	Mercury about 25° ahead of Earth	Promethean phase continues, now positive to the Sun	Mercury turns direct
"Full" Mercury. Superior Conjunction	Mercury opposition Earth	Epimethean phase begins, positive to the Sun	Mercury still direct
Waning Crescent phase some 11 days before inferior conjunction	Mercury approaching the Earth	Epimethean phase continues, negative to the Sun	Mercury turns retrograde

1. The *Promethean-Retrograde* mind is one which seeks its independence from the instinctual nature by opposing it more or less violently. It is a mind which has experienced a "mystery," an "initiation" into a new realm of being—however limited or casual this initiation. As a result, the mind has lost its trust or interest in customary impulses, yet is struggling to get free from them. The mind is "eager," but often bound by the very things it

wishes to forget, or blinded by what it has realized and is "proph-
esying" to the personality and perhaps to all men. However, out
of this inner conflict great personal growth may come, and the
personality may become subjectively identified with a great symbol or image for the actualization of which it is fighting. The
Romantic composer Chopin, the official poet of British im-
perialism Kipling, the Czech leader Edward Benes, faced with the
difficult task of keeping an ideal intact against powerful pressures,
are illustrations of such a type of Mercury-mind.

2. The *Promethean-Direct* mind is essentially established in its
own nature and at peace with the requirements of life. It eagerly
reaches toward the future and seeks to convey the rhythm of
tomorrow to the ego, which may or may not listen very atten-
tively. A few days after the "direct" period begins, geocentric
Mercury stands farthest from the Sun. It is likely to be the time
when the Promethean mind is best able to project its vision in
symbols or in significant patterns of behavior which will serve to
make actual and concrete the Solar potential and purpose. It is
about the time when the heliocentric Mercury is in its "waxing
square" (First Quarter phase) to the Earth. Mental activity is very
intense in a projective manner.

The turning point occurs when Mercury's geocentric speed of motion becomes greater than that of the Sun. At such a time Richard
Wagner was born; and he is a typical example of the Promethean-
direct mind in its most accentuated form—intuitional, inspired,
living in the future. The fact that he had his natal Sun and ascendant
at the beginning of Gemini enhanced his power of formulation. His
friend and sustainer, Liszt, had also the same type of natal Mercury,
slightly past the point at which its speed is greater than that of the
Sun. Napoleon I and the founder of modern Czechoslovakia, Masa-
ryk, are examples of this type of mentality in the field of politics.
Stalin was born at the very beginning of the Promethean-direct
period, while Trotsky was an Epimethean type—which throws a
curious light on the mentality of the two rivals!

As Mercury's geocentric speed increases, it races, as it were, to
meet the Sun in superior conjunction ("full Mercury" phase), and

the Epimethean trend of the mind gradually increases. Mercury's motion is fastest just before or around the time of this superior conjunction; then it begins to slow down. In other words, the Promethean phase of the mind is one in which Mercury's motion is constantly *accelerating*—thus, its "eager" character and its "running ahead of itself." The Epimethean phase is one of *deceleration*, of constant slowing down, of putting brakes on mental exuberance.

3. The *Epimethean-Direct* mind is a "full" mind, by which I mean a mind which seeks to reflect objectively as much as it can of the meaning of life and events after these have occurred. It is the historical, objective mind, which reasons things out on the basis of precedents. It is often the most "successful," practically speaking—not running ahead of the self, or life, but running things and people. When Mercury's motion equals that of the Sun during the "waning" phase of the Mercury cycle, the greatest possible stress on mental objectivity is likely to be made; this is approximately the "Last Quarter" phase of Mercury—which leads to the Epimethean-retrograde period.

Karl Marx is an instance of a Mercury coming close to the retrograde phase, and of a mentality overstressing objective facts and historical analysis, seeking to build the future in terms of historical patterns rather than according to an intuition of new relationships—thus accentuating the factor of determinism. The Epimethean mind tends to be formalistic in its approach to life-relationships and behavior; which may mean "Olympian" at its best (as against the "Dionysian" character of the Promethean mind), or at its worst strictly materialistic and deterministic.

Franklin D. Roosevelt is another instance of the Epimethean-direct mind, with Mercury rising some 16 degrees behind the Sun; and this may seem surprising to some. Apparently his "progressive" tendency was due mostly to his rising Uranus, disposing as it were of his Aquarian Sun, Mercury and Venus—and indirectly of all other planets (except the strong Cancer Moon). His New Deal was based on a clear evaluation of the historical necessity of meeting the far-reaching challenges of a new industrial-technological age. Even the supposedly starry-eyed and mystical Henry Wallace has an Epimethean-direct type of mind, with Mercury at its greatest possible distance from the Sun. In his case the conjunction of Uranus and Sun, and the rising Neptune-Pluto conjunction are responsible for the "mystical" trend, while Mercury shows a very "deliberate" and untrammeled mind. On the other hand, in Cromwell we have the type of Epimethean mind represented by Mercury just past its "full" phase, trying to stamp upon society what it has seen and realized.

4. The *Epimethean-Retrograde* mind is represented by a Mercury coming to a stop in order to be once more fecundated by the Solar will and purpose. In cases like those of Pope Pius XI and of Abdul Baha (whose life was utterly consecrated to the service of his father Baha'u'llah, acclaimed as the "Manifestation of God") we see this type of mind developing along religious lines. In the cases of Benjamin Franklin and of the politician-scientist-philosopher General Smuts, the mentality is found to be of a philosophical character. In both these categories the mind is seeking introspective union with an inner reality; returning to source, as it were. The sense of tradition may be very strong, but it is a means to an end. The mind is not contented with dead-letter worship of the past; there may be a poignant feeling of social discontent, a realization that one should dig underneath, and against the pressure of social patterns and orthodoxy, and thereby be renewed in spirit and in truth.

These four basic categories of mental activity (even more than mental "types") can only give to the astro-psychologist valid indications if they are related to and modified by numerous other factors to be found in the natal chart. To say that F. D. Roosevelt's mind was Epimethean-direct may seem to be saying little about his overall character and destiny; or to call Queen Victoria's mentality (according to Marc Jones' classification) "deliberate and untrammeled" does not tell apparently very much concerning her temperament as a woman and a queen. Nevertheless, what it tells is very essential in any real psychological evaluation of individual character and of defects or tensions in the temperament. In the case of public personages many factors tend to confuse or to throw into exaggerated relief their mental traits; but the astrologer who seeks to understand more fully himself and his problems, as well as his clients, will find the study of the Mercury cycle a most important key to the mental life.

This cycle does not serve only to analyze the character of the natal Mercury—the basic mental temperament—it can be used in tracing the development of the mind throughout the life of an individual. This is done by studying the progressions of Mercury in the ephemeris at the usual rate of one year per day following birth—and also *preceding* birth in the case of converse progressions, less used but often quite revealing of "Karmic" compulsions. We saw already that the years when the progressed Mercury turns direct or retrograde are signposts of the greatest importance. The conjunction of progressed Mercury and progressed Sun are equally significant, as they show change from a Promethean to an Epimethean polarization, or vice versa.

This writer, as a creative artist, had a revealing experience of what such a change may mean. Born when Mercury was direct and rising as morning star some 28 degrees ahead of the Sun (maximum distance), at the age of forty-three he faced a superior conjunction of his progressed Sun and his progressed Mercury on Taurus 15°. Now, since the age of 16 he had been a composer of music, as well as a writer along philosophical and cultural lines. But as the time above-mentioned came near, the focusing of the creative attention along the line of music had to be dropped, for a number of reasons; and a few months after the progressed conjunction of Sun and Mercury, he started to work in an entirely new direction, as a painter.

The significant point here is that music is an essentially subjective and dynamic art-expression, indeed the most Promethean of all arts. Painting, however, stresses objectivity, form and concreteness of meaning. Indeed the change from music to painting had a profound meaning; a sense of inner discovery, as if a new part of the brain and a new facet of personality had begun to operate, was experienced. Yet, because the mental foundation of the natal Mercury remains always a basic factor, the type of painting accomplished still expressed definitely Promethean elements; thus, it was an intuitional type of painting dealing with nonrepresentational, so-called "abstract" and broadly symbolical forms. And some critics insist that it has an inherent "musical" quality.

This personal instance was mentioned only because the contrast between music and the plastic arts is quite expressive of the difference between the Promethean and the Epimethean minds. It might be added also that in this case there has been no change of direction in motion with regard to the normally progressed Mercury; but the changes from Mercury direct to retrograde and again to direct *in converse progressions* i.e. calculated backward in the ephemeris from birth) have been highly significant.

These changes in the direction and polarization of the mental life can be made use of in mental readjustment and mental healing. Every psychologist facing a new client should know whether he or she is close to such a period of mental transformation, for it is only by *working with* the Mercury tide that the best and most permanent results can be accomplished. This is obviously not always possible, but then Mercury is never the only factor to be considered! In many cases the main disturbances in the mental life are related to the Moon, rather than to Mercury. What is then primarily stressed is a problem of bio-psychological adjustment to everyday life at the level of the feelings.

The relationship between Mercury and the Moon has indeed been studied already in modern astrology; and Marc Jones has established psycho-mental differences in temperament by combining two factors: 1. Whether Mercury at birth is morning or evening star. 2. Whether the natal Moon is faster or slower than its average speed of 13°10'. A fast Moon identifies an emotional temperament whose "feelings run high," one might say; or rather which rushes eagerly to meet life insofar as personal day-by-day adjustments are concerned. A slow Moon characterizes a personality which tends to hold itself back and to approach the contests of life with relative cautiousness and perhaps even with overwariness. The four possible combinations of these two lunar types with the two basic Mercury types produce four fundamental types of overall adjustments to life—adjustments which answer to both the need to meet experience in terms of practical give-and-take and feeling-responses (Moon), and the need for maintaining and expanding the substance of one's selfhood (Mercury) through the fulfillment of ever more inclusive social and universal relationships.

Personality is at root the product of the unceasing relatedness of "life" and "mind"—of the solilunar and the Mercury factors, or of parental and social-cultural influences. One may see in this the much advertised interplay of heredity and environment; yet personality is not an expression of heredity and environment, but instead an expression of the functional response of the self to heredity and environment. This expression of the self through the activities of the bio-psychic organism of a human person manifests in the third of the previously enumerated basic functions. This third function deals with self-reproduction and it refers to the planetary pair, Mars and Venus.

IX

An Astrological Key to the Meaning of Sex for Modern Man

THE MANY and varied ways in which frustrations and inhibitions in the field of sexual activity lead to emotional blockages and psychological twists or breakdowns of personality constitute the subject of the most popular phase of modern psychology since Freud. It is doubtful, however, whether the subject of "sex"—in the broad modern sense of the term—is understood in all its implications by most people, including many psychologists. It is not fully understood whenever sex is considered to be always fundamentally a manifestation of the instinct for biological reproduction. The psychological problems referring to sex can indeed never be satisfactorily solved in our day and age unless a distinction is made between the impersonal-instinctual and the personalized-conscious aspects of sexual activity.

Sex is one thing for the man of a tribal and agricultural society whose basic attitude to life and thought are conditioned by the rhythmic processes and the problems of earth production and seed increase. It is quite another thing to the ego-controlled personality of a modern city dweller. To the former, the sex urge is an impersonal manifestation of the tides of fruitful life hemmed in with social-religious tabus. He is acted upon by life as he performs sexual acts. Indeed the real actors in the performance are the male and female cells; the rest of the organism merely supports the essential performers, and whatever psychic and emotional factors enter into the performance are like "overtones" of the fundamental rhythm of universal life. To modern man, on the other hand, sex has become primarily an answer to a personal emotional need; and in this answer individual traits and attitudes are decisive and determining factors, while the strictly biological urge for racial reproduction has become a taken-for-granted, perhaps inevitable, yet often deliberately denied or hated, element.

The development of this modern approach to sex has run parallel to that of the historical process of psychological differentiation and individualization which has transformed the basic character of human consciousness and human responses to life. Human beings have become, in various ways and in varying degrees, individual persons structured by separative, self-conscious, and more or less intellectual egos. They have become so by struggling to assert their independence from the collective tabus of their tribes or societies and from a blind and strictly compulsive subservience to the rhythms of the organic powers of life within body and psyche. This independence, however, usually is of a superficial kind. Its cherished foundations collapse easily when the pressure of basic instincts and glandular activity reaches a slightly unusual degree of intensity. Yet, even though the controls of the ego may be inadequate, the existence of an individualized ego structure is sufficient, not only to repolarize the entire conscious attitude of the individual toward sex, but also to call forth a more or less active and decisive response of the spirit. The ego's development and its self-assertions produce a profound need in the total human being. A host of problems and a series of crises are inevitably experienced. To these the spirit within man has answers, and the one basic answer is the process by which *spirit individualizes itself and becomes incorporated within the structure of the ego, radiating thus through the whole personality.*

This answer is the "incarnation" of the power of divine Sonship into the individual man who has become oriented toward the spirit and an adequate chalice for the spirit's incorporation. By considering the incarnation of Christ into the man Jesus—thus the union of divine and human natures—as a unique event never to be duplicated, because forever sufficient to the wholesale redemption of mankind, most Churches have taken men's attention away from the fact that this process of individualization and incorporation of the spirit into the conscious and differentiated human individual is the one basic fact in the spiritual development of all men. Whether or not the union of God and man in Christ-Jesus was a unique event— perhaps in that it marked the beginning of a vast cycle in human evolution—and whether or not Christ is the "only begotten Son of God," the spiritual fact remains, beyond all theological interpretation and dogmas concerning the nature of Christ, that in every human individual the spirit can *potentially* individualize and incorporate itself, and man has latent within him the "God-seed" within which the spirit can become active in a personalized way.

If this activity of the spirit occurs—and it occurs in answer to the need of the ego, when the ego is ready—a process of incorporation of the spirit begins with what might be called the "germination" of the God-seed within man. And this God-seed, in a general or symbolical sense, is the two-lobe brain (minus the cerebellum which is the "animal brain") with its root-like cerebro-spinal system of nerves (one tap-root, the spine, and many nerve-rootlets branching from it). When spirit becomes truly active at the center of the head, the entire human being gradually changes. It is a very slow change, but one in which the individualizing spirit is the essential factor, and the eventual goal is the full incorporation of the spirit.

Most modern psychologists do not talk about this process. For them, the goal for modern man is to be described almost exclusively in terms of the integration of the personality. But the integration of personality is an *evolutionary* process, reaching from the depths of earth nature to the Sun, from atom to cell, from cell to organism, from primitive to civilized man. On the other hand, the process of incorporation of the spirit, of which I speak here, is an *involutionary* process, a "descent" into man. It is not a rise from depths to heights; or as in the Hindu *Kundalini* Yoga, well known to modern occultists, from the base of the spine and the floor of the pelvis to the crown of the head. It is a gradual conquest and spiritualization of man's total human nature from the head to the feet.

Such a head-to-foot sequence of progressive phases of unfoldment should not surprise the astrologer. Astrology, as we know it
in the Western world, was presumably developed by wise men
(Chaldeans?) who formulated its symbols in order to record for
posterity this very process of incorporation of the spirit. This was
done at a time when, the era of strictly tribal societies being near
its end, the arising of crucial problems caused by the future
generalized growth of the ego and of the intellectual mind in
individualistic societies could be foreseen by men of spiritual vision. As we already stated, the process of incorporation of spirit in
man is the direct answer to these problems; and the sages of old
sought to record in the series of zodiacal symbols the twelve basic
steps in this process.

Every astrologer knows that the first zodiacal sign, Aries, corresponds to the head; Taurus, to the region of the neck, etc. But
what seems not to have puzzled astrologers is the fact that the
sign made to correspond to the sex organs and sexual activity in
general, Scorpio, is an autumnal sign—thus, related to a time
when physical nature becomes dormant in preparation for the
winter sleep. Should we not consider one of the zodiacal signs of
spring (particularly Taurus, a symbol of fertility ruled by the
planet of love and of all seeding processes) as the astrological focus
for all sexual activity, if by sex we mean the biological function of
reproduction of physical organisms? Obviously, the glandular and
chemical activity of sex is stirred in all nature during springtime.
Life moves forth, tearing leaves and blossoms out of stems, stirring love in human bodies and souls. Yet, Taurus is related to the
throat—not to the genitals. What is the meaning of this seeming
discrepancy?

The meaning is, first, that the sequence of zodiacal signs at the
human level refers to the *involutionary* process of incorporation
of the spirit in personality and its radiation in creative works
through personality. What is more, at this truly human level, sex
has a meaning profoundly distinct from that of instinctual biological reproduction, even though biological reproduction is a generic
necessity; a necessity which, however, can be *used* by man as a

vehicle for the expression of personality—either creatively or disintegratively.

If we consider the series of zodiacal signs in terms of the process of incorporation of spirit, we find that Aries, the first phase of the process, represents the "germination" of the God-seed; that is, the arousal in the brain of a new vision and new images under the impulse of the spirit's desire—the desire to experience, to feel and to love, to communicate with others, and through communication to build the foundation of a true communion in spirit of all men. In Taurus, the germinating God-seed sends its roots into the region of the throat; and as this occurs, the power of speech is aroused. Through vocal tones the Word may become incarnate and active among men. In Gemini, the spinal center which controls arms and lungs (the center of the cross of spine and extended arms) is reached by the spirit which then expresses itself in mental activity and in the power to fashion things and to associate images into concepts, words into sentences. And the Cancer phase represents the further incorporation of the descending spirit into personality; that is, into the power to gain full objective awareness of self through a bio-psychic organism.

What the desire of the spirit envisions and images forth in Aries, becomes in Taurus voice and utterance—but *not* sexual activity. Animals are seized by biological urges, whose unconscious compulsion leads at once to sexual acts; but in human individuals who have felt the power of the spirit, biological compulsion is overshadowed by the spirit's desire, which is true love; and sexual acts are replaced by the long courtship expressing itself in the many utterances and the songs of love. These, in a collective human sense, are the substance of all that comes under the term "culture." A truly cultured man is a man in whom the desire of the spirit for life and for love, for human comradeship and beauty, expresses itself in harmonic, restrained and meaningful actions. He does not act in unconscious glandular compulsion and unrestrained haste or excitement; but instead he acts out consciously the vision and the great images that have been aroused within his brain during the Aries phase of spiritual germination.

Needless to say, many human beings do act impulsively as merely earth-conditioned and instinct-driven creatures. They act in terms of glandular chemistry, not of spirit-born culture; in terms of uncontrollable passion, not of the love imagery created by the spirit's desire. Indeed, in the very vast majority of men and women now living it seems that even though a conflict may be experienced between these two alternatives of behavior, the driving energy of blind propagation is still the dominant factor.

Yet the very fact that this purely biological urge in many cases becomes a violent and torturing passion, that human beings are often haunted and maddened by what they call "sex," shows plainly that this kind of sex is no longer the unconscious springtime activity of vegetable and animal nature. Something has happened to it. It is no longer a manifestation of Taurus fertility. A dark torment cries out through it; fear and despair are behind the yearning to lose one's insulated ego in a union with another; it may even become a passion for death through the gates of lust.

This darkness and passion are associated with Scorpio; yet they represent only the negative aspect of this sign. Scorpio symbolizes "human" sex—sex as an expression of personality, as a release of the power generated by the establishment of an individual, and at least relatively isolated, ego. It is only because this ego is often not able to bear its isolation and loneliness, because it is tortured by a sense of inferiority, fear and insecurity, that its expression in and through sex is permeated with anguish, jealousy, possessiveness and lust. Sex, then, is not a creative expression of personality, but instead an escape from personality, a form of suicide of the ego; and therefore sex can become, as lust, the gate to the "black path" of self-destruction—the more so, the more spirit has been aroused into activity within the structure of this ego.

This arousal of the spirit does not mean that all problems are henceforth solved! The descent of the spirit into the human organism *can* end in spiritual defeat, if the energies of earth-nature overwhelm its rhythm and distort its character. Defeat may indeed be experienced by the spirit at each of the twelve basic steps of its incorporation in the bio-psychic personality. But one of the most dangerous steps is probably that represented by Scorpio, for it is there—in the realm of conscious and personalized sex—that (at the present stage of evolution of most human beings) the ego lets go of the self and turns negative in a critical manner.

Men are as yet so basically insecure and lonely as individuals that their egos are dark with fear and anxiety. In *personalized sex this fear and anxiety are released,* under whatever form they originally took in the early development of personality—escape from self and inner weariness, jealousy, greed, boredom, a sense of guilt, etc. Yet, if the ego had not been formed under the pressure of insecurity and as a result of a violent, passionate severance from the wombs of family, religion, society, then sex would mean the release of the creative strength of the ego. If it had this positive significance in the life of personality, the spirit, in its process of incorporation and "descent" into the total personality, would then be able to experience one of its basic powers in and through sex *consciously and creatively used.* Scorpio could become the field for the creative expression of an integrated personality transfigured by the spirit, and no longer a whirlpool destroying whatever energy of an insecure, defeatist and tragic ego is caught by its vortex—as is so often the case in our day and age.

Scorpio is the fifth sign in the zodiacal sequence beginning with Cancer, and the fifth phase of any life process of the type studied in astrology can always be said to carry the meaning of "self-expression"—creative or destructive—as can be seen from the traditional characteristics of the fifth house in the usual type of birth chart. Scorpio refers thus to the self-expression of whatever originates in Cancer, and Cancer has the meaning of a *focus of integration within strictly defined and conscious boundaries.*

For the man who has emerged from the womb of family and tribe this focus of integration is the ego. It is an individualized field of consciousness structured by the definite realization "I am this particular person with this particular individual character." Most civilized men today have become, in varying degrees, individual personalities. However, used in such a way, the term "personality" refers to the end-result of an evolutionary ascent from the roots of generic nature. It is the fruition of a particular culture, a particular society, in response to the challenges of a particular geographical and psychical environment. Thus one can say that humanity is expressed in personality; human nature aspires to and blossoms forth in the individual person (cf. C. G. Jung, "The Integration of the Personality" p. 281).

This, however, is not the only possible meaning of personality. The word means etymologically "an actor's mask" (persona) as used in large theatrical performances in ancient Greece and Rome. These masks were meant not only to portray in strong outlines a definite emotional expression or type of character, but also (because they contained a small mouthpiece) to carry the actor's voice farther. Personality thus can mean an instrumentality for the release of something. It can mean an agency for the activity of the spirit. This involutionary instead of evolutionary meaning is the one meaning to be considered as we deal with the zodiacal process of individualization and incorporation of the spirit. Spirit takes concrete form in personality. It descends into the structure of the ego, the integrated field of individual consciousness; and, as this descent (or "birth") occurs, the consciousness, the ego and the entire earth-born personality eventually become transfigured. If this descent of spirit into personality takes place in the symbolical Cancer, then the release of the creative power of this transfigured personality can be said to occur in Scorpio (fifth sign after Cancer). This possibility reveals the essential, spiritual meaning of Scorpio, once the negative traits of the ego have been "redeemed" and transfigured by the incorporation of the spirit within this ego. It points to what could be the spiritual or spirit-conditioned reality of sex in individualized and conscious human beings.

We may not, from this, grasp as yet very clearly what the goal is—i.e. the full spiritual meaning of Scorpio—yet we should be able to see the direction in which the descent of the spirit must seek to reorient man's conscious attitude toward sex. Only through such a reorientation can modern man's basic emotional problems be solved, at least insofar as these are rooted in sex.

The goal of the creative release of the spirit-illumined personality in Scorpio can be understood in a general sense by realizing that the ninth sign after Scorpio is Leo. And what does Leo symbolize if not "solar" man; that is, an individual from whom the spirit radiates forth in conscious splendor! Leo is the child of spirit, and this spiritual progeny is a conscious progeny. It may take the form of an actual child, whose parents were able to endow with a radiant spirit-polarizing psychic organism as well as with a healthy body; and it may also be the "Christ-child within the heart" of Christian mystics, the "Diamond Body" of Asiatic occultists—a body of light, vehicle of spiritual man's immortality. At whatever level this creative act of the spirit-illumined personality be focused, the outcome is a "work of the spirit." Spirit has created a progeny through a conscious, individualized and consecrated personality; while in the case of the merely biological and instinctual kind of birth, it is the compulsive and "blind" power of life that operates through unconscious bodies.

This distinction is basic. It gives the one essential key to a really convincing and effective understanding of the problems disturbing, and often shattering, the emotional lives of most modern men and women. These problems arise because humanity—at least the most advanced portion of it—is now being reoriented and repolarized from the level of compulsive and unconscious life processes to that of consciously individualized and inherently free (because self-determined) acts in and through which the "inspirited" personality expresses itself and releases its powers. This reorientation of human activity presupposes clear consciousness and at least the first stage of the individualization of spirit. It presupposes an ego. If the ego is oriented to the spirit in positive self-assurance and in the security that can only be founded upon faith and the love that is of the spirit, then, this ego becomes the "temple of the living God"—or at least the scaffolding making the erection of this temple possible. But if the ego is filled with fear and anxiety, poisoned by the toxins of a violent emergence from the psychic wombs of family, religion and society, then it finds itself compelled to unburden its fears, or to seek an escape from unbearable loneliness and weariness, through dark or meaningless, brutal or frantic attempts at sex-expression.

Modern man's sexuality is conditioned by the character and quality of man's ego. The ego is the source; sex, the outflow into

whatever the ego is able to envision as the purpose of its being—
or, so often alas! the purposelessness of it. The emotional life of
the individuals of our day is conditioned by these two foci: ego
and sex. Around them, in most cases, it whirls in disharmonic and
unstable ellipses; and its orbit is strewn with ghosts and frustrations, with the torturing of futility and tragedy. The only hope
for peace and truly creative harmony is spirit-illumined understanding.

♈ ♉ ♊ X ♋ ♌ ♍

Mars, Venus and the Emotional Life

♎ ♏ ♐ ♑ ♒ ♓

THE SIGNS of the zodiac over which Mars and Venus have been given "rulership" in traditional astrology constitute a most significant indication of the meaning and direction of the two basic aspects of the emotional life of civilized man. One of these aspects refers to spring; the other, to autumn. Mars and Venus are said to rule the beginnings of both spring and autumn; that is, Aries-Taurus and Libra-Scorpio. But while Mars rules over the first sign and Venus over the second sign of spring, Venus rules over the first sign of autumn, Mars over the second. This reversal has a deep as well as very practical meaning. It reveals the difference between vernal life and autumnal life; the former originating in Martian impulsiveness, the latter characterized by the in-drawing power of Venus which establishes "magnetic fields" within which activities of one kind or another are integrated. The products of these activities are released through some new channels at some future springtime.

The essential qualities of spring and fall are focused in the two equinoctial moments: the first point of Aries and Libra. The former is characterized by a Martian *emergence* from the "womb" of the collective life of humanity—represented in symbolism by the sea, the place of emergence of life on our planet. The latter (the first degree of Libra) signifies the fixation in the until then separate personality of those traits and qualities which constitute the archetypal and immortal nature of every human being—his divine Sonship. Libra begins thus the first stage in a process of *transfiguration* of the individual personality, at the end of which the latter becomes a perfect likeness of its Creator, the "God-Elohim" of the first chapter of Genesis in the Bible.*

Martian emergence and Venusian transfiguration constitute the two poles of the unfoldment of the individual personality of man. Man's emotional life is polarized by these two trends or forces. He is urged to discover and realize his self as an emergent and separate individual person, structured by an ego whose "center of gravity" or focus of consciousness is the feeling, "I am I, this particular and unique person"; and he is urged also to recognize within his personality those essential or archetypal characteristics, at first latent and unconscious, which constitute the seed-pattern of his divinity—a divinity which he holds in common with every man and which represents his likeness to the Creator-God.

Before a man can realize the meaning and recognize the image of this divinity-within that he has in common with every other man at the same level of individual unfoldment, he has to accept the fact that in him also there are many biological-psychological traits and features which are common to all men, and particularly to human beings who are his kin in race and culture. Thus "man's common humanity" must be recognized before "man's common divinity" is to be realized as a vital reality within—before the Venusian birth of the Living God (the symbolical Christ-child) can take place within the heart and soul of the individual person.

In Libra, the individual recognizes his social, cultural and spiritual kinship with other men; first with a particular commu-

---

*This creator is not to be confused with the "Lord-God," Jehovah or Yahveh, who makes his appearance only in the second chapter of Genesis and who "forms of the dust of the ground," but *does not* "create," man. The distinction is an essential one, without understanding which the real nature of man and of the evolution of the human personality can never be recognized. God-Elohim "creates" archetypal man, Christ-man; the Lord-God, Jehovah—a tribal God—fashions only physical or Adamic man. As the Christian mystics all pointed out, man must "die to Adam before he can be reborn in Christ." This rebirth begins at the symbolical fall equinox and it implies an equally symbolical "death," or sacrifice of the separative will of the ego.

nity and culture, then with the whole of humanity. In Aries, on the other hand, man seeks to go forth into the wide world, intent above all upon proving his self to himself—that is, upon projecting and expressing this individuality he feels stirring within him. Yet this individuality is still at its first stage of emergence from some kind of collective womb claiming its undivided allegiance—a family, a tribe, a binding religion, an ancestral culture. Mars-ruled Aries represents a motion outward into space; Venus-ruled Libra, a motion inward toward some common reality. Mars is the first planet outside of the earth's orbit; thus a focus for all outward-going expression. Venus is the first planet inside of the earth's orbit; thus a focus for all attempts at reaching center. Mars is the gateway to outer space; Venus, the gateway to the Sun. Man's emotional life oscillates between the paths leading through these gates.

This oscillation is a normal and spontaneous movement. It becomes abnormal when obstacles on these paths thwart, frustrate or deviate the flow of the energy of being and the realization of the outward and/or inward desires of the individual soul. Then tensions, cramped attitudes, fears and defeatism, and the ultimate result, a complex, develop. Back of this complex one should be able to trace characteristic peculiarities of innate mental attitudes, and, even more, of emotional functioning.

Mars and Venus are the main astrological symbols—and some astrologers would like to say, the determining factors—of the emotional life; that is, of the way in which the reproductive energies of life and the desires of the individual soul operate, seeking expression and satisfaction. We said that these desires act in two basic directions: outward (Mars, as ruler of Aries) and inward (Venus, as ruler of Libra); but this obviously means little unless we grasp more fully the nature and substance of the desires themselves and their relationship to the functional urges of biological reproduction. This we may do if we realize that the drives or urges which operate characteristically in living organisms in early spring during the symbolical Aries phase of the zodiac can be defined by the term "germination." Aries is the symbol of all germinative processes; and this, not only at the biological, but also the psychological and even cosmological, levels. And *germination presupposes a seed.* It is the bursting forth of the substance of the seed, and the release of the energies contained therein—substance and energies spreading outward according to some plan (or pattern of organic growth) mysteriously inherent in the seed.

Science has shown that there is no generation of life "out of nothing." Even if an organism could be "materialized" without a normal process of germination from a seed or fecundated ovum, there would still be some kind of metaphysical seed as its foundation at the mental-spiritual level—an Image projected with occult power, a *logos* impregnated with divine creative energy. These too have to "germinate" before they can manifest concretely at the level of physical expression; and Mars is always the source of the germination power. This source is essentially desire— whether we speak of the cosmic desire-to-be of spirit in answer to the need of matter for a new chance to become integrated in the likeness of God, of the desire of an animal for its mate, or of the desire of an individualized human soul for self-expression or for reintegration in some socially or spiritually encompassing community.

In *our* astrology, the yearly cycle of the zodiac begins with the appearance of new life-forms; thus with the germination process in Aries. But the germination that begins the new cycle presupposes the seed that came at the apex of some preceding cycle—and I should add, not always the immediately preceding one. Venus rules over all seed and seeding processes; but this Venus is surely not Venus as ruler of the "feminine" sign, Taurus (its "night house" in medieval terminology); a sign which *gives substance to* the process that began in Aries. It is autumnal Venus, ruler of the "masculine" sign, Libra—the sign which sees, symbolically at least, the completion of the seeding process and the release (fall or harvest) of the seed from the plant, or from any other organic Whole at whatever level it be.

It is said traditionally that "behind will stands desire"; i.e. that man can only exert his will in terms of what he desires. But one must go still further: man can only desire what he has learned

(whether through education or through self-discovery) to value.*
Thus, the autumnal Venus rules the first and fundamental phase
in the development of the sense of value. Culture and ethics in
any human collectivity, individual character in any single person,
proceed from such a sense of value. This sense unfolds through
the period Libra to Pisces—passively in kingdoms below man and
in primitive man, actively in those men who have truly become
individualized or, symbolically speaking, who have consciously
become the "seeds" of their own future cycles. It is on the basis of
these Venusian factors—sense of value, seeds, etc.—that the
Martian germinative impulse operates in Aries. Autumnal Venus, thus, determines the character of being (whether at the level
of the biological species, the social collective culture, or the conscious individual vision and purpose); vernal Mars, the desire and
capacity for *self-expression* (be this self collective or individual),
that is, for the actualization of character, vision, ideal, value in
concrete living.

In biologically productive sex (focused in Taurus) the essential
actors are male and female seeds, spermatozoon and ovum. The
desire is actually centered in the generative organs themselves.
The desire is primarily of the endocrine glands, hormones and of
seed, and only secondarily, superficially, or even not at all, of the
conscious individual soul. On the other hand, where we deal with
a *personalized and conscious human expression of sex* (thus with
Scorpio), desire is fundamentally of the individual soul or at least
of the organism-as-a-whole; and this desire is not essentially a

---

*Some might claim that a man may desire what he knows is worthless; but in
such a statement the man that desires and the man that knows are actually two
different personalities, and the statement simply reveals the fact that there is an
internal split in the individual. The part that desires the so-called worthless
object or event actually feels it to be of great (though perhaps tragic and compulsive) value. He may know that, at some other time, other and perhaps contradic-
tory goals or objects have seemed to him to have greater value, yet, as the act
occurs, the value of the desired object toward which the act is directed must
appear great and significant to whatever it is that directs the act.

desire for outward action (though there be muscular action and movement seemingly outward), *but a desire for psychological communion and for the concrete expression of Venusian "value."*

In the majority of cases, sex is in civilized modern man the result of psychological, far more than biological, causes. It is a desire for human communion (and often an escape from individual selfhood and a sense of tragic isolation) far more than a desire for self-reproduction in a progeny—whether the participants in the sexual act admit it or not.

These facts should be fully taken into consideration if one is to orient himself in the mazes, complexities and frustrations of modern man's emotional life. The analytical psychologist sees the results of frustrations, fears or degenerative processes in the "body-mind"—the total personality—of his clients. His tendency naturally is to focus his attention upon the fact that psychic energy (the so-called "libido") has been dammed and repressed into the subconscious (Jung's "personal unconscious") where it turns corrosive or explosive—thus the popular idea that if only this repressed libido were allowed to flow freely, all would be well. The careless vulgarization of Freud's approach to the problem fails obviously to take in consideration the fact that this Martian libido (the term simply means, in Latin, "desire") *is itself but a result, not a cause.* It is the outflow of something from somewhere. What must be discovered is not only what happened to the outflow (where and how it was dammed, why it dried up, etc.), but even more what occurred at its source, *at what level* this source is primarily located, and what type of factors operate at that level.

This, the astrologer can do, at least in a general way, by considering first the natal Venus of the individual—also progressions and transits referring to it—then, his Mars; lastly by studying the relationship between these two planets as it exists in the natal chart and as it develops through progressions and transits. The natal positions themselves are to be seen as phases of a particular cycle that began, before the person's birth, with the last conjunction of these two planets. In other words, no separate judgment

on either Venus or Mars makes much sense insofar as a real
understanding of a person's emotional life is concerned. The two
planets are to be studied together—and also in relation to the
Saturn-Moon pair which always tend to crystallize into psychic
entities (complexes) whatever disturbances there may be in the
Venus-Mars coupling.

I shall discuss presently the few basic astrological indications
concerning the way in which the Venusian and Martian functions
operate in a personality; but it seems necessary at first to establish
more clearly the meaning of these functions and the original
quality of their activity.

Venus and Mars are the two planets immediately surrounding
our Earth, and they symbolize indeed the most intimate factors in
the personal life—the immediacy and spontaneity of being,
whether "being" is understood at the generic and biological level
or in terms of individualized and psychological selfhood. If we
consider Jupiter and Saturn, we have to deal with a type of human
activity which is motivated by some kind of established relationship and which is meant to fit somewhere (Saturn) and to assimilate or overcome something (Jupiter) in order to fit better and
more successfully. Saturn, as symbol of the Father image, represents the sense of security, because he who feels that he fits well
in society is secure, and it is normally through the father's activities that the child finds himself placed in a particular relationship of class, wealth and occupation to society—while he finds in
his mother (Moon) an example (successful or not) of the ability to
adjust oneself to this "place" defined by the Saturn-father. But
what is this "oneself" that is to adjust itself to the social place,
traditions and culture represented by Saturn? What is the individual child to start with? What makes a man act naturally and
spontaneously the way he does, without any reference to place or
function within an established group, simply because he is what
he is?

However much materialist thinkers may believe that heredity
and environment condition utterly a man, few are those who will
refuse to admit that there is in every human being an element of

personal freedom and of pure spontaneity of being, however weak and ineffective. There is a realm in which man feels "I am I," and from which he seeks to move outward in sheer self-expression toward whatever appears to him good, valuable and fulfilling. This realm of intimate being is the realm of Venus and Mars. Venus establishes the character and essential quality of the intimate and direct realization of selfhood and value. Mars is the desire and ability to act it out, with no reference to any other factor except insofar as this factor helps or opposes the individual act. What should be called "the emotional life" is a twofold manifestation of this immediate sense of individual being and of the desire and effort to express it in acts.

It should be clear that the emotional life thus defined operates at three levels. At the *biological* and generic level, the emotional life is a manifestation of organic being and glandular activity; it rests upon the harmonic or disharmonic condition (Venus) of the organs, glands, and systems of the body—and this condition or state determines the possibility of release (Mars) of hormones, fluids, and also toxins within and outside of the organism.

The same twofold operation is found at the *social-cultural* level with reference to the activity of collective feelings and collective ways of thinking, insofar as the collective factors are taken for granted and implicitly, unquestionably accepted as an integral and intimate part of one's self—thus, insofar as the self is identified with them. For instance, the feeling of "original sin" and of the wickedness of human nature, the thought that men who are not baptized are heathens, are collective factors so intimately believed in by the typical Puritan, that they color the character and quality of the very sense of "I am I" (Venus) as well as the immediate spontaneous responses of the self to life (Mars).

Then there is the level of the truly *individual* soul, at which man realizes his intimate selfhood in terms of the values (Venus) he has discovered and chosen as his own, and acts accordingly as an individual (Mars).

Venus and Mars can operate at all three levels in one particular individual. In many cases they do operate at these three levels simultaneously, and there may be conflicts between the values established at each level, because the personality is not well integrated—that is, the values established at one level do not determine the total behavior of the personality, at least at any particular time. This shows how difficult it is to make a complete and reliable psychological picture of any individual's emotional life from a study of his birth chart; for, even if it be granted that the meaning of Mars and Venus (and related astrological factors) is well understood in their particular natal setup (plus progressions and transits), the difficulty remains of estimating at what level the personality is normally centered, at what level Mars and Venus operate usually—and, what is more, operate under any particularly stressful life situation.

On the other hand, the astrologer has this advantage over the ordinary psychologist that he can know the basic character of the Venus and Mars function at any level and under any circumstances. To know this does not give the astrologer the ability to *predict accurately* what the person will actually feel and do at any particular time—no one should ever forget this point!—but it gives him the ability to *understand more fully* why and how the person feels and acts as he or she did, or is about to do. And such an ability in turn can become a foundation for wise judgment and helpful suggestions; which is all any astrologer should ever attempt to pass on to anyone asking for his help.

XI

Venus in the Natal Chart

IF I attempt now to sum up the contents of the preceding chapters I shall state first of all that behind every desire to act and to express one's self in an outward manner (Mars) there is some kind of value, incentive, directing image or feeling—psychological factors which all refer to the Venus function. Symbolically speaking, Mars refers to the process of "germination" at all levels, and germination presupposes a "seed." Venus rules over all "seed," whether it be the concrete seed of biological organisms or some corresponding factor in the realm of psychological, mental and spiritual activity. Just as a few basic seed-ideas, archetypes (Jung) or prime symbols (Spengler) are to be found at the origin of every culture and religion, so every individual person is determined in his behavior (Mars) by a few basic images, feelings or personal *leit-motives* which he has built within his psyche as the result of early life experiences. If these crystallize and acquire a compulsive, unconscious or semi-conscious power, they take the character of psychological complexes; but even if they remain adjustable and influenced by new experiences and greater knowledge or wisdom, they are still the power behind the throne of the ego, conditioning the individual's desire for self-expression in outward acts.

Venus, as such a positive behavior-determining factor in man's inner life, is related mainly to the zodiacal sign Libra (her "day house") and to the fall equinox, the symbolic time at which the mature seed is released from the plant that bore it. Venus, as ruler of the spring sign Taurus (her "night house") is, on the other hand, subservient to the positive Mars-in-Aries, the energy at the core of the vernal equinox period. Venus is then that which gives substance to the Martian impulse and outward initiative. It is the woman who "bears children to" her man and concretizes his desire for self-extension into a progeny. Thus, generally speaking, Venus in the early vernal signs of the zodiac is largely dependent upon the Mars function which gives it direction and purpose; it is Venus as an instinctual power of fertility. But when placed in autumnal signs, Venus acquires a very positive determining energy which dominates, for good or bad, the emotional life.

The dualism of autumnal and vernal polarities, which finds expression in the zodiacal position of Venus, is not, however, the only dualism which can be associated with the Venus function. Both ancient mythology and traditional astrology have considered Venus as a star-performer in two alternate roles; as evening and morning star—Venus Hesperus seen in the western sky immediately after sunset, and Venus Lucifer in the eastern sky at dawn, herald of sunrise. In astrological terms, Venus Hesperus is a Venus whose zodiacal longitude is *greater* than that of the Sun (for instance, Sun in Libra 0°, Venus in Libra 10°). Venus Lucifer is Venus with a longtitude *less* than that of the Sun, thus *rising ahead* of the Sun.

It is unfortunate that so little attention has been given to the double role of Venus, except perhaps by astrologers dealing with alchemical symbolism. A great wealth of significance can be found in this Venusian dualism if it is carefully related to a psychological study of the emotional life—and, most likely, also to that of glandular activity in the physical organism.

Venus Lucifer, as morning star "rising ahead" of the Sun, refers to a type of emotional activity which might be said symbolically to run ahead of the self. This does not mean necessarily an extroverted or especially intense or unrestrained type of emotional life—even though it often tends to have such a general meaning. It describes originally a person who goes out to meet the world (and especially other human beings) with an eager expectancy as if life itself depended upon the results of the meeting; nevertheless, if this expectancy has been shocked and turned into a sense of profound disappointment, the person may seem to be externally cold and retiring—a coldness which is only a mask of self-protection.

Venus Lucifer is represented by the quality of feeling of adolescence. The antennae of the feeling-life are stretched out to the utmost. There is a basic sense of personal insecurity, and the feelings are primarily depended upon to serve as guides and signposts. In later life, these feelings may be given the more mature and respectable name of "intuitions"; yet essentially the nature of the process remains the same. The individual "feels" situations and persons in an act of almost immediate ethical judgment. They are good or bad—for him and at that particular time. He acts as he *feels* he must act, and there often emanates from him a strong contagion of feelings, a "warmth of feelings." In this class we find the following names taken at random: Walt Whitman, Richard Wagner, Van Gogh, Jean-Jacques Rousseau, Napoleon I, Mussolini, Maria Montessori (the gread educator), F. D. Roosevelt—and the U.S.A. birth chart.

Venus, as evening star, is a symbol of *feeling after the act;* that is, of the type of emotion which results from and is a judgment upon an action having been performed. This kind of judgment is usually a graded one; the action has been a "test" and the wise-man-within-the-soul sits in judgment and gives to the man-of-action a "grade" after studying the case. The judgment is either esthetical (it considers the value of the relationship between all significant factors in the case) or legalistic (thus according to traditional standards and precedents).

Venus Hesperus might be called theoretically an indication of greater emotional maturity or wisdom; but actually, this "maturity" may be that of the "change of life," a time when an individual's complexes catch up with him and induce a crucial psychological crisis. Indeed many persons with Venus rising after the Sun may be highly emotional, but this emotionality is not as spontaneous and immediate as when Venus is morning star in a birth-chart. It is a tense, perhaps passionate and at times destructive kind of emotionality—because, when there is excess or violence of emotional activity, this excess or violence is the secondary result of frustrations and fears.

In other cases, Venus Hesperus indicates a type of emotional life strongly influenced by traditional and cultural or spiritual values—the emotional life of aristocratic men and women. A list of well-known persons born while Venus was an evening star would include George Washington, Jefferson, Woodrow Wilson, Wilkie, Henry Wallace, Eisenhower, H. P. Blavatsky, Francis Bacon, Einstein, Winston Churchill—and, as well, the charts of England and of the United Kingdom.

An interesting example of the distinction between Venus Lucifer and Venus Hesperus is given by the chart for the Declaration of Independence and that for the time when the Constitution was adopted *de facto* as a result of being ratified by nine States (June 21, 1788). In the former, Venus is morning star; in the latter, it is far "behind" the Sun. The Declaration of Independence was adopted in a mood of emotional intensity and heralded as a yet-unrealized reality; but the process of formulating and ratifying the Constitution involved a long-drawn-out discussion and judgment as to the value of federalism. However, in the Inauguration chart of April 30, 1789, Venus is again morning star. The period of discussion was ended, a new beginning was made, a new "feeling ahead" toward self-expression as a national unit under an executive head.

Venus as morning star is the power which builds "magnetic fields" and archetypes; that is, which gives form to the spiritual release of solar energy, source of all manifestation—not however, a concrete, physical form, such as belongs to the realm of Saturn, but an archetypal-spiritual pattern of energy, a web of electromagnetic forces. The individual with a strong natal Venus Lucifer normally seeks to project his "vision and purpose" upon life; to impress the rhythm of his essential being upon society. He feels himself a herald, a mouth-piece of God. He pours his self emotionally and often proudly into his creations. This emotional outpouring may be neutralized by other factors in the total personality—other planets or negative aspects to Venus; still, even if frustrated, it can usually be detected as a characteristic element.

Individuals born with Venus as evening star may be in appearance just as "emotional" as those with Venus as morning star; but, where it is so, one can find usually some basic inferiority complex or mother-complex against which the person reacts in an aggressive manner, or by a forced type of creative outpouring. A typical case was Theodore Roosevelt whose natal Venus rose behind the Sun, but whose personality was stamped by the power of an opposition of Mars rising to the Moon, and by an elevated Sun in Scorpio. Venus in Sagittarius was also opposed by Jupiter and squared by Neptune (both planets being retrograde); and Venus stood on the cusp of the 12th house. Add to these the fact that Saturn squared the opposition of Pluto to a Sun-Mercury conjunction, and you have a pattern revealing extraordinary tensions. Teddy Roosevelt was able to release the power which these generated and thus avoided being destroyed by them, but such a release carried the mark of aggressiveness—the "big stick policy."

When Mercury rises ahead of the Sun and Venus behind the Sun, Mercury can often substitute for the "Luciferian" aspect of the Venus function. Mental pride, tinged with emotionalism, replaces the typical emotional pride of the Luciferian ego. Emotions are used as a means to an end by the mind, because a basic sense of emotional insecurity may forbid the spontaneous "warmth of feelings" of the typical Venus Lucifer. Indeed it may be hard to separate what is of the mind and what of the emotions in any analysis of personality; but, by studying carefully the relative positions of Mercury and Venus with reference to the Sun the astrologer can orient himself in the maze of a complex psychological nature far more safely than the usual psychologist who sees only empirical results—what his client tells him, what he can detect in his appearance and behavior—but not the primary structural pattern of the personality (the natal chart).

Another kind of dualism is revealed by an astrological study of the Venus function, according to whether Venus' motion in the sky is "direct" or "retrograde." I have previously discussed the meaning of the direct and retrograde motions of the planets and stated that this meaning is fundamentally derived from the fact that a "direct" planet moves in the direction of the Sun and Moon (symbols of the bi-polar life force), a "retrograde" planet against it. I also pointed out that a retrograde natal Mercury does not indicate a weak, dull or lazy mind, but a mind which operates basically in counterpoint to the instinctual nature and the flow of the life-force. When Mercury is retrograde one finds that the vital drives or impulses of the Sun and the most characteristic trends of mental activity are in contrast, perhaps in conflict; yet this state of affairs can be the very condition required for spiritual growth or personality-development at certain stages of evolution of the permanent Identity of the individual.

The same type of analysis applies to the case of Venus retrograde; with this difference, however, that Venus and Mars are retrograde only for a short portion of their synodic cycles. The average cycle between two *superior* conjunctions of Venus and the Sun last 584 days (about one year and seven months), and its retrograde phase—during which the *inferior* conjunction occurs—only about six weeks. This is the shortest time a planet spends being retrograde relatively to the length of its complete cycle; which means that it is rarer for a person to be born with Venus retrograde than with any other planet retrograde.

This fact must obviously be significant if there is any value whatsoever in astrological symbolism. Psychologically speaking, it refers primarily to the close connection there is between the life-force and the emotions. Venus and Mars represent the most immediate and intimate manifestations of the personal life, the realization in feeling and the expression in acts of the "I am I, this particular and unique person." And if Venus is symbolically the source of this sense of "I," the life-force that streams forth originally from the Sun is the "Am" that gives substance and reality to the "I." To feel alive is a requirement for the realization of "I"—at least in terms of earthly existence.

Nevertheless there are cases in which this sense of "being I" develops, as it were, against the instinctual flow of the vital forces of the human organism. There are people whose sense of value runs counter to their natural instincts; people, for instance, who are born with the tendency to be ascetics and to fight against the normal demands of their organs and glands; people who seek to curb and perhaps annihilate their spontaneous sense of being individual souls, either because of the urge for self-transfiguration and holiness, or because of their becoming a prey to powerful disintegrative forces that tend to destroy the sense of spiritual Identity in any individual. It is to these and other psychological conditions that Venus retrograde in a birth-chart refers.

A significant illustration is provided by the chart of Annie Besant, first an advocate of birth-control, then a prominent Theosophist and President of the Theosophical Society with headquarters at Adyar, South India. Mrs. Besant was born in England, October 1, 1847, with a Libra Sun in the 6th house, behind which came a retrograde Venus. Mars in Taurus (1st house) is also retrograde, and Uranus retrograde is rising in Aries. Saturn and Neptune are also retrograde, Mercury in Libra is direct, but rising behind the Sun (i.e. Epimethean), Jupiter is direct and conjunct the Moon in the 1st house and Cancer—thus squaring the Aries-Libra planets.

Such a chart suggests the strongest possible kind of "ascetic" type; that is to say, a person whose emotional and social life is founded upon self-denial and rebellion against tradition, whose life energies are bent inward under the sway of a tense Uranian will for self-transformation. Venus and the Moon are, however, exceedingly strong by zodiacal positions and aspects; the feelings are very intense but working under conditions of constant psychological crisis. All positive values are given to the mental functions (Mercury and Jupiter are the only direct planets—besides the Sun and Moon which are always direct); but Mercury and Jupiter are in square, and Uranus exactly opposes Mercury. The Sun had just set at birth; the fall equinox (the yearly "setting" of the Sun, one might say) had recently occurred; and birth occurred in a lunation cycle bounded by two eclipses.

Annie Besant's long crusade for birth control is an illustration, at one level, of her opposition to the natural flow of the life-force. Later, as a Theosophist, she combined a passionate eagerness for spiritual transfiguration and "occult" powers, and a dramatic desire to serve selflessly humanity and "higher Beings," with a great deal of mental pride. Indeed, she was an extraordinary personality symbolized by a very unusual type of birth-chart.

A very different chart is that of the French President, Charles de Gaulle, who became the living symbol of the greatness of his nation. In it also we find Venus retrograde and evening star—and the General's deeply mystical temperament was well known. Here we find a man whose emotions were set in a mould thoroughly defined by a national and religious tradition; a man without much personal warmth but with an almost compulsive devotion to a cultural ideal which made of him the symbol of his nation.

The English astrologer, Alan Leo, was born also with Venus (and Mercury and Mars and Neptune!) retrograde; Venus, however, was morning star. He was a Theosophist and profoundly influenced by the occultist's approach to life. He helped considerably the renascence of astrology in English-speaking countries and thus the spread of a type of values and thinking which ran against the trend of the English 19th century civilization.

The position of Venus (geocentrically calculated) can never be more than 47 degrees distant from that of the Sun—making then a semi-square aspect to it. After reaching this distance to the Sun, Venus, which has already begun to slow down, comes gradually to a stop and retrogresses, making a loop in the sky. At inferior conjunction Venus is found at her closest proximity to our earth, and thus near that time glows with her greatest brilliancy; then the planet turns direct again and speeds away from the Sun in the zodiac, reaching her greatest speed (around 1°15′ per day) after the superior conjunction, i.e. when the Sun is between her and our earth.

I mention these astronomical facts because the difference between the two kinds of conjunctions of Venus to Sun is not only one of the *direction* of Venus' motion, but also of the *speed* of this motion. At "inferior conjunction," Venus is not only retrograde but slow—and also close to the earth and near days of great brilliancy. At "superior conjunction," Venus is direct and as fast as it ever can be. The usual astrological textbook simply speaks of "conjunctions of Venus and the Sun," as if all conjunctions had the same meaning. This is obviously not so, at least at the psychological level. One should also realize that as the most distant aspect between Venus and the Sun is the semi-square (45°), the relationship between these two great astrological factors in a birth-chart cannot be defined primarily by the "aspect" they make to each other. Only two of the usually acknowledged aspects are possible, the semi-square and the semi-sextile (30°).

The former may be called a discord, the latter a concord; yet to say this does not give enough light upon the natural relationship between the Sun and Venus—and this is a basic relationship where the study of the personal life and the feelings is concerned. It is for this reason that the distinction between Venus Lucifer and Venus Hesperus is so important, and it is wise to add to the study (in close psychological analysis) the more subtle characteristics derived from the speed at which Venus moves at the time of birth—and also perhaps (as Charles Jayne has suggested) a consideration of whether this motion is accelerating, "decelerating" (becoming slower) or maintaining its speed.

In conclusion it seems important to add some remarks which refer to Hitler's nativity because many astrologers have been reluctant to admit that Hitler could have Libra as his rising sign, Libra having the reputation of being a "harmonious" sign of the zodiac. However, the basic truth of astrology is that *every* factor in a chart can be either positive or negative, constructive or destructive. In fact the totalitarian ideal is "harmonic" inasmuch as harmony literally means the process of becoming one. The totalitarian state aims at unanimity, but this unanimity is of a negative kind and is based on the ruthless exclusion of all that refuse to be coerced into unity. Hitler's character was eminently Libran in a negative way; but his planetary ruler, Venus, was retrograde, in conjunction with Mars in Taurus, and in square to a 10th house Saturn in Leo. A very "strong" Venus indeed according to the usual astrological way of measuring the strength of the planets, but a strength turned *against life*.

The Sabian symbol for the degree of Hitler's Venus-Mars conjunction (Taurus 17°) is: "A symbolical battle between 'Swords' and 'Torches' " (Tarot cards.) Here then we find focused the battle between might and enlightenment which has been rending our humanity at the threshold of the immense possibilities which the Industrial Revolution—and now atomic power—have opened. The whole emotional and personal life of the Fuehrer was concentrated on that point; he became the symbol of this struggle for millions. The violent character of the way he solved the problem for himself and the world can be seen in the fact that the retrograde Venus was just about to fall, as it were, into Mars' arms: a surrender of "values" to "violence," of the "inner" to the "outer."

The conjunctions of Mars with retrograde Venus are special features of the cycle of the Mars-Venus relationship. At every fifth conjunction of Mars and Venus, Venus is retrograde, and this occurs about every 77 months. These special conjunctions have moreover a cycle of recurrence in the same zodiacal sign (with a lag of about 7°20') of nearly 32 years. They mark indeed moments of great intensity in the emotional life of humanity. At these times, men should be able to reorient their sense of values and their emotional attitudes, to repolarize their feeling of "I am I" and sow new seeds of action.

Hitler did this, in his own way—a dark way. Thirty-two years after his birth, Mars and Venus retrograde once more met in Taurus (April, 1921). The German Worker's Party had been organized a year before. Hitler was on his way to power, as the old cultural structures of Germany were being dissolved by inflation. Anything might have happened—even a great spiritual metamorphosis. What did happen is now past history.

XII

Mars in the Natal Chart

MARS IS the first planet outside of the earth's orbit. This, plus its red glow and other associations of ideas, has made of it, in astrological symbolism, the focal point for all releases of energy and all renewal of activity originating in man's "earth being"— that is, in the body and in the aspects of the personality which are conditioned by the energies and processes of life on earth. Mars is the symbol of muscular activity and, beyond it, of the many and varied desires or drives which compel or urge man to move, i.e. to change any static position of equilibrium he has reached.

As spirit's essential characteristic is harmony and equilibrium, whenever spirit is seen to move from a less inclusive to a more inclusive condition of integration the operation of the Mars function must be the cause of this change. This means, in more concrete terms, that if a person is at ease with himself and the world *within the framework of a particular attitude to life and to society*, some Martian impulse will have to operate if he is to grow into a wider viewpoint and a more inclusive condition of mental-spiritual balance—a broader consciousness of life and of his own selfhood. This Martian impulse will necessarily produce at first unbalance, dissatisfaction, restlessness, and at last some outgoing type of activity. When a man desires to touch an object, because he is urged to include the feel of that object in his consciousness of the outer world, he has to move a muscle. The act of walking is the act of moving toward or away from an object, and this act consists in a series of falls and quick recoveries from falling. Mars causes the falls; Venus, the recoveries from falling. Every step a man takes in walking implies the operation of these two basic life powers.

This is true of all forms of activity. To act is to become unbalanced. It is to fall from a condition of balance, of peace, of self-contained satisfaction or serenity. Such a Martian centrifugal (i.e. away from center) trend must be sooner or later followed by a Venusian centripetal (i.e. toward center) impulse, or else the individual experiences a complete fall, which only the resistance of the surroundings (the floor, the ground) ends, and may end with destructive results. This is true whether the Martian outward desire expresses itself in a physical act, or in a psychological emotion ("e-motion" meaning a "moving outward").

Mars is thus the adversary of the *status quo*, of peace and rest—and of all limited and particular kinds of equilibrium. Therefore he was understood in ancient mythologies not only as the god of war, but, wherever a religion appeared as a justification and deification of some established social order, as the adversary of spirit. Yet the Mars function *of itself* should not be considered as the original cause of the outgoing impulses of life. If a man desires strongly enough to touch any object so that he is impelled or compelled to tense some of his muscles and to move toward this object or psychological goal, it is because the object has acquired, at least for the moment, a value of some sort. Man desires only what he values at the time more than what he has; and the sense of value is a product of the Venusian function, either alone or (in most cases) in association with the Mercury function which refers to the memory, to the faculty of association of images, to concepts and all similar mental factors.

Indeed, Mars should be considered normally as the servant of Venus and Mercury, in so far as Mars rules over the *mechanics of action* (muscles and will, etc.) which express and actualize outwardly the mental and emotional directives given respectively by Mercury and Venus, especially when these planets are found rising before the Sun (Mercury-Prometheus and Venus-Lucifer). Yet there are numerous cases in which desire and the impulsion to act outstrip the feeling of value, and perhaps run riot. Muscular tone or tension is so high that the muscles must move, regardless of what they move for. The secretion from the adrenal glands which controls the capacity of the muscles to operate may be so abundant that a man "itches to do something," and that anger— an uncontrolled release of negative emotion—flares forth, compelling usually destructive action. Likewise a nation may have built such a strong army or navy and given so much power to their General Staff that the latter presses constantly for war, whether or not the people feel the value or logic of any aggressive step and of the goals which such a step might secure.

In other cases, the contrary is the norm. The power to move forth aggressively, and even to take relatively peaceful personal initiative in any situation, is very weak. The individual cannot drive himself to act, because of organic weariness and muscular lack of tone, or because of Mercurial mental conflicts and confusion, or the inability to see more value in one thing than in another (Venus function.) It is often difficult for the consulting psychologist to discover at once which is the primary cause and which the effect; and this is where natal astrology (also progressions and transits) may be of great assistance to psychological analysis. The strength or weakness of Mars and the related characteristics of Venus and (less so) of Mercury may show at once where the focus of disturbance is to be found.

When indications of strength or weakness in the Mars function refer only to the usual astrological evaluation of the position of Mars in this or that sign of the zodiac according to the traditional concepts of rulership, exaltation, debility or fall, no particularly stressful psychological problem can be deduced. A natal Mars in Libra or Taurus may be as normal and healthy, psychologically speaking, as one in Aries or Scorpio. Psychological difficulties are the results of either certain types of relationship to other planets, or retrogradation, or special emphasis due to position in natal Houses. And even then, one must always remember that psychological or physiological difficulties, *when overcome*, are the sources of strength and of new abilities.

The classical example of a Mars function complex is the birth chart of Freud, founder of psychoanalysis (May 6, 1856, around 9:17 a.m.). In it, everything stressful happens to Mars, yet Freud achieved great fame and was the fountainhead of a vast movement with endless repercussions in all cultural and social fields. The intense focalization upon the Mars function, under every kind of pressure and strain, gave Freud his creative power; and the chart stands as a typical symbol of Freudian "depth-psychology" and of the historical reaction against the frustrations and perversions which European society, and especially the Victorian era, had imposed upon this Mars function.

In Freud's birth chart Mars retrograde on Libra 4° is placed at the Nadir of the chart, the only planet below the natal horizon. It is in opposition to a 10th house Jupiter, in sesquiquadrate aspect (135°) to Uranus and the Sun in mid-Taurus, and in square to Saturn. It is in trine to the Moon, the only trine in the chart but the Moon is in semi-square to Venus in Aries, and the Sun in semi-square to Saturn and to Jupiter, the square of which it bisects. Mars is also in 150° aspect (quincunx) to Pluto on the 11th house cusp.

From the standpoint of traditional astrology Mars retrograde in Libra would be estimated "weak" and, considering all the "bad" aspects it makes, very destructive in a somber and deeply insidious manner. To say this, however, would not explain Freud and his individual genius. I once wrote that Freud's birth chart is a surgeon's knife piercing relentlessly and cleaning out the abscesses and tumors in man's deep subconscious, letting loose the poisons produced by man's social shams and repressions built up through the Piscean Age (Neptune and Jupiter are in Pisces). This is the chart of a scavenger of the psyche. It could have been that of a criminal or of an incurable psychotic, except that the focusing of Mars energy is so spectacular as to suggest the possibility of all this power being used in a remarkable manner. It was used by Freud, strictly speaking, in a "destructive" manner; but it was destruction at the service of a *potential* greater health. Freud was the greatest of all "muckrakers" of the turn of the century; he exposed, not society's sores and economic abuses, but the evil in man's social attitude (Libra)—an evil generated basically by man's relationship to his parents (Mars is in the fourth house), or

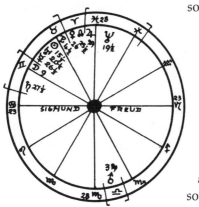

rather by the intellectual and social products of such a relationship when inadequate, thwarted or discordant.

The T-cross linking Jupiter, Saturn and Mars is characteristic of the tensions created by social values and traditions, and poisoning the very sources of the emotional-sexual life. Freud, as a Jew, suffered numerous abuses and ostracism of a sort. His father (Saturn at the 12th house cusp) was presumably to him the symbol of society's condemnation, while his mother (Moon trine Mars) must have been stressfully loved. We should note also that Mars and Venus are "in mutual reception;" i.e. Mars rules the sign in which Venus is placed (Aries), and Venus the sign in which Mars is placed (Libra). This gives a peculiar strength to the emotional nature, and no doubt helped Freud to overcome and to *use* his complexes. The power to use them is suggested by the revolutionary, but inspirational, Sun-Uranus conjunction, and particularly by the quintile of Jupiter and the Moon, ruler of the chart. The sextiles of Neptune to Sun-Uranus, and of Venus to Saturn, gave Freud also the power to significantly organize unusual psychological materials.

For Marc Jones the planetary gestalt of the chart belongs to the Bucket Type, already mentioned. To me, it is a characteristic example of a Wedge (or Funnel) pattern, Mars being the cutting edge of the wedge, or the opening through which the power of the concentration, in spring zodiacal signs, of planets within the broad square of Neptune (Pisces 20°) and Saturn (conjunct the star Betelgeuze on Gemini 28°) is released with dramatic intensity through an autumnal Mars.

Here, we have actually a paradox, for the spring signs of the zodiac refer to the spontaneous flow of the desire for life and of the procreative urge—the *libido* of Freudian psycho-therapy. Mars normally is the channel for, and indeed the substance of this *libido*. But Mars in Freud's chart, is not in a spring sign; we find it instead at the fall equinox, and what is more, retrograde, i.e. moving "against the grain" of the solilunar life forces. The vital energies of Freud are at high tide in a condition of springtime release; but that which makes the release possible—viz. Mars—is oriented, most stressfully, in a direction which opposes release! Obviously the inner conflicts in the founder of psychoanalysis must have been acute. If an inner explosion were to be avoided there *had to be* a release. What kind of a release? The only possible one was one that would shatter the very social conventions and sense of values associated with Mars' zodiacal sign, Libra. Freud had to be an iconoclast, a breaker of idols. His terrific Martian energy had to alter the Martian thrust of the male *libido* so as to transform it into the surgeon's knife. This is the way such a strong complex can be used and made to serve a social purpose. Destructiveness has to be oriented toward reform, and thus be made a servant of life and God.

In some cases, such a natal chart might well suggest some severe physiological handicap. But the Sun is "hyleg" (i.e. symbol of health and stability) in Taurus; and a Mars retrograde is often an indication of stubborn vitality. It certainly does not mean, of itself alone, a "weak" body; though it may reveal at times some abnormal condition in Mars-ruled functions.

Though a planet retrograde indicates theoretically a function whose activity is directed against the natural flow of life energies, the term "against" does not mean necessarily in a state of enmity. When, in a musical motet, two voices move in counterpoint, one going up in the scale while the other moves by descending steps, this does not mean that the two fight against each other, but instead that the two motions are *complementary*. Thus by a process of "opposition," each supplements the other.

Another example: If two men starting from London want to

study the earth's globe along the circle of London's latitude, it will be quicker for them to move in opposite directions, one to the east, the other to the west. As they meet at the antipodes of their starting point, they will have covered between them the entire circumference of the globe. As they exchange the results of their experiences, they both reach a "global" viewpoint. *On a globe, opposite directions converge.*

Retrograde planets go in a direction opposed to that of the Sun and the Moon, but by so doing they can accomplish what has not been previously accomplished through direct motion. They are able to repair the sins of omission and commission performed during the periods of direct motion. If they move against the grain of the life forces it is so as to solve the problems left behind the ever onward moving flow of evolution and of time. It is to repair the damage done by life experiences, when these experiences were frustrated by complexes or thwarted by social shams and prejudices.

To live means to face constant challenges of adjustment to new conditions; challenges which are caused either by inner growth and expansion, or by changes in the surroundings. Man, individually and collectively, rarely meets such challenges so well as to leave nothing unsolved. Toxins and heavy memories accumulate in the depths of the personality as the by-products of even normally successful activity. Thus in many instances it is necessary to clean the instruments and tools required for action after the action is performed. It may also be essential for a man to retrace his steps, to try again what was done badly, to go over the past in order to understand better what did actually happen. To learn from life means to assimilate fully the harvest of experience, and to reject nothing in fear or confusion. What is so rejected falls into the pit of the subconscious, there to fester and decay.

The retrograde period of the planets are times for us to go over the past, to clean our minds and souls of waste materials, and to repair whatever harm has been done to them—and perhaps to adopt a new way of using power, a new technique.

The retrograde periods of Mars are particularly important because Mars is the power to act and to move forth into the world, away from our center; and many of the most crucial troubles or evils in society and in the personal lives of men come as the results of misuse of this Martian power of desire and initiative. These retrograde periods, however, are different from those of the "inner" planets, Venus and Mercury, inasmuch as at the center of them Mars is in opposition to the Sun, and not (as in the case of

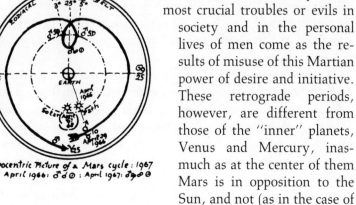

Geocentric Picture of a Mars cycle : 1967 = April 1966: ♂ ☌ ☉ : April 1967: ♂ ☍ ☉

Venus and Mercury) in conjunction with the Sun. This is a most significant fact, psychologically speaking. In terms of the inner life of mind and feeling (Mercury and Venus, respectively) the solution of man's need and the power to repair his sins of omission or commission is to be found in a new approach to—a conjunction with—the solar center of life and selfhood. But, where the power of desire and of outward motion are concerned, what is needed to repair the mistakes and solve the problems caused by subjective involvements in outer objects or persons is *objectivity and perspective*. And these are the results of a planet's opposition to the Sun, such as is typically demonstrated by the full Moon.

In other words, if anything has gone wrong with the Mars function or if it has failed to operate at all, the time to readjust it and to solve the problems it has led to is when Mars is in opposition to the Sun; for then (astrologically speaking at least) Mars is fully illumined by the Sun and the meaning of all it represents can be seen with the utmost objectivity. As I said above, this Mars-Sun opposition is the center of the retrograde period of Mars, and it is the key to the meaning of the entire period. In Freud's case birth occurred toward the close of such a Mars retrograde period, and the opposition of Mars to the Sun had taken place more than one month before (April 2) on Aries 13°, close to the April New Moon on Aries 16° (April 5)—a solar eclipse, at the time of which Mercury, Venus, Jupiter and Neptune were conjunct in Pisces in square to Saturn.

It can be said that the first half of the retrograde period of Mars up to the opposition of the Sun is a preparation to this climactic point. It is mostly after the opposition has occurred that whatever has been gained or realized then can be made to serve a progressive purpose even though it was seemingly at first a destructive (or rather cathartic) process. Depth psychology is a psychology of ego catharsis; it seeks to cleanse and purify the psyche or inner life of the individual from the waste products of a discordant and hectic or frustrated and deviated type of personal activity.

The psychological approach featured in the writings of Adler stands in polar opposition to the approach of Freud. It is most interesting therefore to find that in Adler's chart Mars is direct and in conjunction with the Sun, while, around this conjunction, Mercury and Venus are seen both retrograde. Adler's main problem had to do with his inner life of thinking and feeling, with his sense of value. On the other hand, he relied upon an impetuous and self-glorifying Mars (conjunct to the ninth house Sun in Aquarius). His "inferiority complex" was based on a sense of *frustrated values:* he felt inferior, and reacted against it by a "superiority complex," ego bravado, and a philosophy of forced optimism and self-assurance. In Freud, on the other hand, the main problem was due to *frustrated desires.* He did not feel basically inferior, but rather thwarted by society and traditions. He was a rebel, whose violent revolt was turned into valuable channels as a cathartic, cleansing force.

In studying the meaning of Mars retrograde in a natal chart, or of an entire Mars retrograde period in relation to transits and to world events, significant indications can be obtained from the important aspects—especially conjunctions—which Mars may make while being retrograde. These aspects show, quite clearly in most cases, the type of energies which can be used in the process of reorientation of the Mars function. The planets forming aspects are those which will, or should contribute the most to this process—or at least they indicate what has to be done in order to achieve the purification and repolarization of the Mars function.

Mars had formed trines and oppositions with Mercury and Venus, while being retrograde before Freud's birth, but otherwise had made no conjunction with any other planet. The one spectacular feature of the period was Mars' opposition to the solar eclipse above mentioned, which therefore stands as a key to the process of Martian reorientation at the time. It occurred before Freud's birth, and hence we may consider it as a reference to his ancestral or spiritual past, that is, as a "karmic" or residual factor in his deep unconscious and that of his race and culture.

Mars is retrograde during less than a tenth of the time elapsed between two of its successive conjunctions with the Sun (about every 25 months). Thus approximately, in every ten persons one is born with Mars retrograde. Obviously therefore too much cannot be deduced from such a position; yet it is infrequent enough to establish very definite characteristics in so far as the emotional life and the quality of the ability to express one's self are concerned.

The "1001 Nativities" gives many cases of Mars retrograde, and at least one of them is that of a criminal, another that of a Pope (Pius V)—totally different personalities obviously. Yet in all of them the psychologist could no doubt have found some complex, some basic frustration of the life force, which would have been the key to the unusual character of their emotional, and perhaps biological, temperament.

XIII

The Urge to Self-Transcending

EVERY LIVING organism undergoes constant transformations, but normally during a single span of its existence a tree or an animal experiences organic changes which follow a set generic pattern of growth, maturity and disintegration. This pattern can be modified in the course of the evolution of the species. There are organic mutations, but, at least as far as we are able to know, the individual organism (a particular plant or animal) is not conscious of the possibility of transforming itself, and especially has no conscious desire or yearning for a transformation which would alter radically the conditions and the awareness of its existence. This organism does not plan or will to become superior to what it naturally and generically is.

It is man's privilege, and in a real sense his awesome responsibility, to be capable of altering radically the conditions of his existence through the use of a mind which presents to him new possibilities and unprecedented ways of acting. Man can always become a greater being. There is in this human mind a power that seeks to bend every circular process of thought into a spiral; and there is also in the human organism something—we may call it the heart or soul—which is capable of yearning for basic changes in feeling, for new ways of relating to other living entities and to the universe as a whole.

When we studied the first three basic drives of organic existence we found ourselves in a realm where things not only are what they are, but seek to remain and reproduce what they are. This takes place at the physiological level of the body, and also at

123

the level of an organized society and of an individual person. In any case we are dealing with activities occurring within definite boundaries and according to more or less set patterns and schedules. Saturn, Jupiter and Mars refer to such activities. Saturn symbolizes the formative power within all structural factors. Jupiter represents the feeling for social fellowship and the urge to a collective integration of human activities *within* the structural patterns imposed by Saturn, so that each person may find life easier and more abundant. Mars refers to the outgoing activities of a physical body and an individual person—activities which are guided by either generic, collective-cultural, or individual judgments of value (Venus).

The basic goal which these drives seek to reach is, broadly speaking, happiness in well-being—i.e. in being pleasantly and abundantly what one is. "What one is" is this often elusive "identity" for which we are told today we must search, a search which seems to confuse so many of our young people. It has become a confusing search because the Saturn-Jupiter functions in modern society and in the prematurely individualized modern youth do no longer operate satisfactorily; that is to say, the basic structures and the sense of interpersonal relationship along well-defined traditional lines have shown themselves to be obsolete because ineffectual under our new conditions of existence.

What produced these new social and personal conditions? The fact that the power latent in man's mind and "soul," to which I referred a few paragraphs above, has enormously increased its activity—viz. The power to transform radically the very foundations of our thinking and our feeling-nature. The causes of such an increase can be explained in various ways. We have apparently reached a new phase in the process of human evolution, and we are living through a period of transition between the old phase which is gradually passing away, and a new one the character of which is as yet uncertain—an uncertainty productive of widespread social disturbances and personal anxiety.

This period of transition, interestingly enough, has seen since its beginning the discovery of three planets beyond Saturn's orbit,

Uranus, Neptune and Pluto—and it is probable that at least another planet will be discovered still farther away from the Sun. Thus everything has happened as if, when humanity needed new symbols to identify the newly aroused powers within its mind and soul, it found these planets in its field of vision; that is to say, it discovered means to deal more consciously with, and to measure these new powers.

The powers, of course, had been there all the time within Man; but they had not been used *collectively and consciously*—i.e. in terms of publicly acknowledged social, cultural and personal values—to the point of becoming life-and-death issues *for humanity as a whole*. They had operated mainly, if not exclusively, through especially sensitive and evolved pioneers, through "mutants" (we might say) in whom the vast, impersonal driving power of evolution—or some will prefer to say, the Will of God—was able to operate under unusual conditions.

Even in the India of the Upanishads the yogis and mystics constituted a small minority, and how few have been the individuals who truly lived a Christ-like life? Once Christianity became an organized religion it entered the realm of Jupiter and Saturn; it became a social factor. Yet there is no doubt that the revolutionary changes in human consciousness, which now have reached a high and perhaps critical level were foreshadowed by developments which started at least as far as the sixth century B.C. It is not impossible also that the existence of Uranus and Neptune was known to some of the priest-astrologers of Chaldea and other countries, for they probably had means of investigation of super-physical character.

However, by studying the cycles of conjunction of the three trans-Saturnian planets we can conveniently and significantly identify and measure some of the most important rhythms of history and of the evolution of civilization all over the globe; and I am referring particularly to the nearly 500-year long cycle of the Neptune-Pluto conjunctions (the last one having occurred in 1891–92 early in the sign, Gemini) and to the cycles of Uranus and Neptune, or Uranus and Pluto.

Here, however, I shall only mention a few points which refer to
the pair Uranus-Neptune and are especially relevant to the subject
of this book, leaving a vast amount of material concerning the
three trans-Saturnian planets to be dealt with in another volume.* Uranus and Neptune constitute indeed a closely related
pair, in that they represent in the type of astro-psychology I am
presenting the two aspects of the function of self-transformation
and self-transcending, at least in its preliminary manifestations.

A Saturnian world is a closed, circular safe world—a world of
endlessly repetitive processes. Uranus makes of it an open field in
which "ex-centric" (centrifugal) forces either persistently or
periodically win over "con-centric" (gravitational) habits and a
conformistic tradition-worshiping mentality. Uranus' victory
may be explosive, if the resistance of Saturnian entrenched in-
terests and concepts is too great to allow any compromise or
give-and-take. But Uranus is not necessarily the advocate of revolutionary violence. It represents the centrifugal push that, if
not stubbornly resisted by the concentric pull of Saturn, acts at
every point of a cycle, transforming circular into spiral motion—
i.e. motion that harmoniously and beautifully expands from
center outward, as is shown in a perfect spiral, such as nature
shows us in the shape of a seashell like that of the nautilus.

Alas, in this world of earth-matter and at this present stage of
human evolution, harmonious transformations toward the state
of open, ever-expanding selfhood are very rare, for the products
of man's mind (concepts, institutions, religions, etc.) possess a
powerful inertia—i.e. a resistance to change. Thus Uranus has,
most of the time, to act where there are strongly disturbed areas
and emotional pressures in a human personality, or when a society is passing through an acute crisis (war, defeat, economic de-
pression, collective fear, etc.). The action of the Uranus force
upon the critical area of the personality or the society tends as a
result to be explosive; yet in most cases this action has become

---

The Sun Is Also A Star: The Galactic Dimension in Astrology (Dutton and
Co., New York. 1975)

acceptable to the more aware parts of the personality (or the society) which nevertheless may be suffering from and fears the spread or intensification of the disturbing factors.

The same is true with regard to Neptune; but this planet deals with the realm of feelings and values rather than with the mind and its traditional concepts or personal blockages. Feelings too can be constricted or totally blocked by fear and anxiety; values can be frozen up into a rigid state in which any suspicion of change causes a tight ego-shell to close up until the danger to the *status quo* appears to be past. Complexes are generated which it is the function of Neptune to dissolve, or, in many cases, merely to elude.

What Uranus has shattered, Neptune then dissolves. It is the "universal solvent" of the alchemists. But Neptune refers also to all means a human being uses to escape from unbearable repetitive Saturn-controlled conditions; for instance, home drudgery, assembly-line factory work, monotonous form-filling typing, etc. Boredom and a depressive state of feelings result from such repetitive activities *unless* the performer can feel deeply within himself their value, that is, unless he accepts them wholly because they serve a high purpose which he has truly made his own. Boredom and a sense of futility generate a yearning for escape. This desire can lead, in time, to psychotic states; but at first we see it active in drinking, drug-taking, compulsive traveling and fun-seeking or love-making, and in many forms of pseudo-mysticism or supposedly "cosmic" consciousness.

Neptune in this negative aspect is the escape into formlessness, irrationality and meaninglessness. It acts wherever man by some intoxicating *glamor* abdicates from his individual selfhood. In its positive aspect, however, Neptune refers to the vision of a realm in which forms are "open" and all-inclusive, and to the deep faith a person has in the possibility that he or she may be of real service in helping to make actual on this earth the sublime (or subliminal) realities of such a transcendent and trans-Saturnian realm.

Uranus and Neptune should work together in making possible the transition between todays dominated by Saturnian yesterdays and creative moments utterly dedicated to glowing tomorrows.

But often they do not, and this generates not actual complexes, but negative answers to complexes (or social-cultural crystallizations). Complexes, however, do develop when a naturally strong Uranus-Neptune function of self-transformation has become repeatedly frustrated. As we have already seen, this may produce a "sense of guilt" which can poison the soul and distort the mind.

Negative forms of Uranus-Neptune activity can occur also when the great vision of a Prophet, a true mystic, a creative pioneer in one field or another, becomes materialized and so formalized that it loses all its radiant openness to life and to the tide of universal change. As the vision materializes into an organized religion (or any rigid social-cultural institution) it falls into a condition of subserviency to the Jupiter-Saturn purposes. This is more or less inevitable at present, but it calls in due time for the relatively violent operation of the too long inactive Uranus-Neptune function.

With Pluto a state of more or less total denudation of the personality is reached. Pluto atomizes all substances, reducing them to their most primitive elements. It lays bare all the stagnant depths of human nature, punctures all the unconscious shams, destroys all glamor, renders escapes futile and sickening. But it does all this—symbolically speaking—so that the seed it holds preciously within its realm (the beautiful "Proserpine") may find rich humus for its growth when the springtime of a new cycle begins.

Everything, indeed, in life serves an ultimate purpose and contributes to the everlasting Harmony of universal existence—even the most stubborn complexes and the deepest fears or emotional tragedies; for they are needed to polarize, when the time comes, the most intense activity of the transforming powers of life.

The activity of these powers becomes more understandable and predictable to the wise student of astrology, as he or she studies the cycles of Uranus, Neptune and Pluto in the lives of individuals and nations. Through such an activity, man experiences the mysterious process of metamorphosis at the end of which he reaches the full actualization of the potentialities so long hidden within his innermost seed-being. He becomes not merely a greater human being, but "more-than-man." He becomes one with the "star" that is his spiritual essence. His consciousness no longer depends upon the Sun for bio-psychic sustainment, for he has become a participant in the Brotherhood of Stars, our immensely vast Galaxy.